ANIMAL EXTREMES

BIGGEST BODIES

BY MARISSA KIRKMAN

WWW.APEXEDITIONS.COM

Apex is distributed by North Star Editions:
sales@northstareditions.com | 888-417-0195

Produced for Apex by Red Line Editorial.

Photographs ©: Shutterstock Images, cover, 1, 4–5, 6, 7, 8–9, 10–11, 12, 13, 16–17, 18, 19, 20–21, 21, 22–23, 24, 25, 26, 27, 29; The Natural History Museum, London/Science Source, 14–15

Library of Congress Control Number: 2022919860

ISBN
978-1-63738-526-5 (hardcover)
978-1-63738-580-7 (paperback)
978-1-63738-687-3 (ebook pdf)
978-1-63738-634-7 (hosted ebook)

Printed in the United States of America
Mankato, MN
082023

NOTE TO PARENTS AND EDUCATORS

Apex books are designed to build literacy skills in striving readers. Exciting, high-interest content attracts and holds readers' attention. The text is carefully leveled to allow students to achieve success quickly. Additional features, such as bolded glossary words for difficult terms, help build comprehension.

TABLE OF CONTENTS

CHAPTER 1

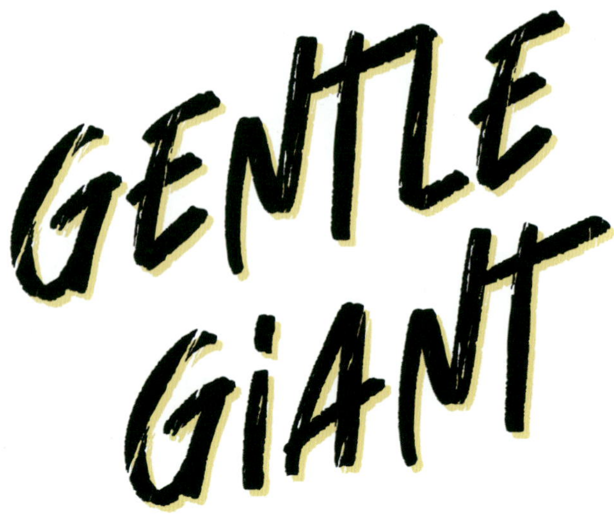

GENTLE GIANT

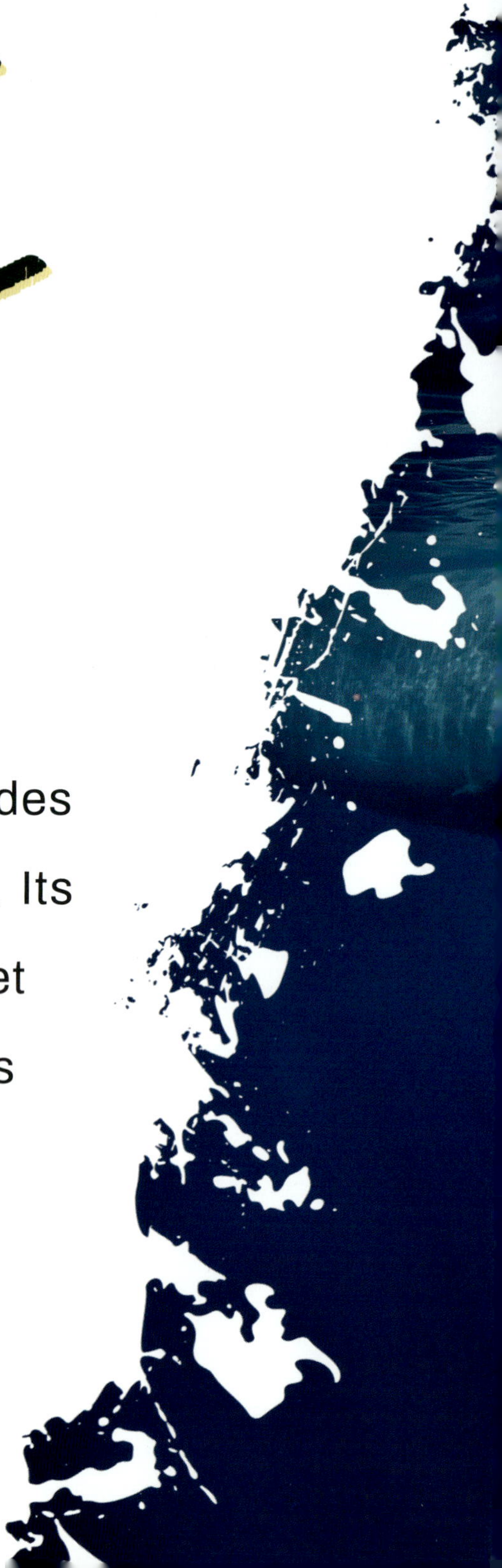

A **massive** whale glides through the ocean. Its blue-gray body is 110 feet (34 m) long. And its tail is 25 feet (8 m) wide.

Female blue whales are often bigger than males.

The whale lifts its large head out of the water to take a breath. Water sprays from its **blowhole**.

A whale breathes through a hole on the top of its head.

On average, blue whales grow 80 to 100 feet (24–30 m) long. That's about as long as six cars parked end to end.

EARTH'S LARGEST ANIMAL

The blue whale is the longest animal in the world. It is also the heaviest. Blue whales can weigh more than 330,000 pounds (150,000 kg).

The whale flaps its huge tail. Its **calf** swims beside it. The baby whale is already 23 feet (7 m) long. And it will continue to grow.

Whales sometimes stick their tails up out of the water.

CHAPTER 2

BIGGEST IN THE WATER

The blue whale is the largest animal in the water. But other whales come close. For example, fin whales can grow 85 feet (26 m) long.

Fin whales live in cold and deep ocean waters.

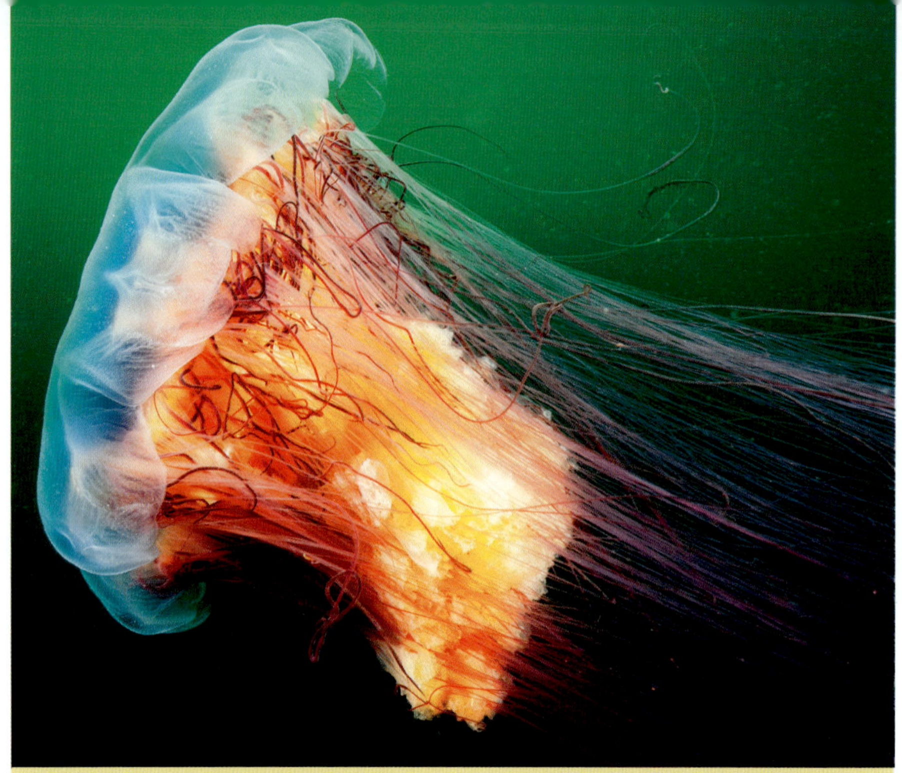

A lion's mane jellyfish uses its tentacles to catch and eat food.

The lion's mane jellyfish is the longest sea creature. Its **tentacles** can grow 120 feet (37 m) long.

LARGE SHARK

The world's biggest fish is the whale shark. This shark can be 40 feet (12 m) long. And it can weigh up to 20,000 pounds (9,000 kg).

Whale sharks have large, wide mouths. They eat tiny sea creatures.

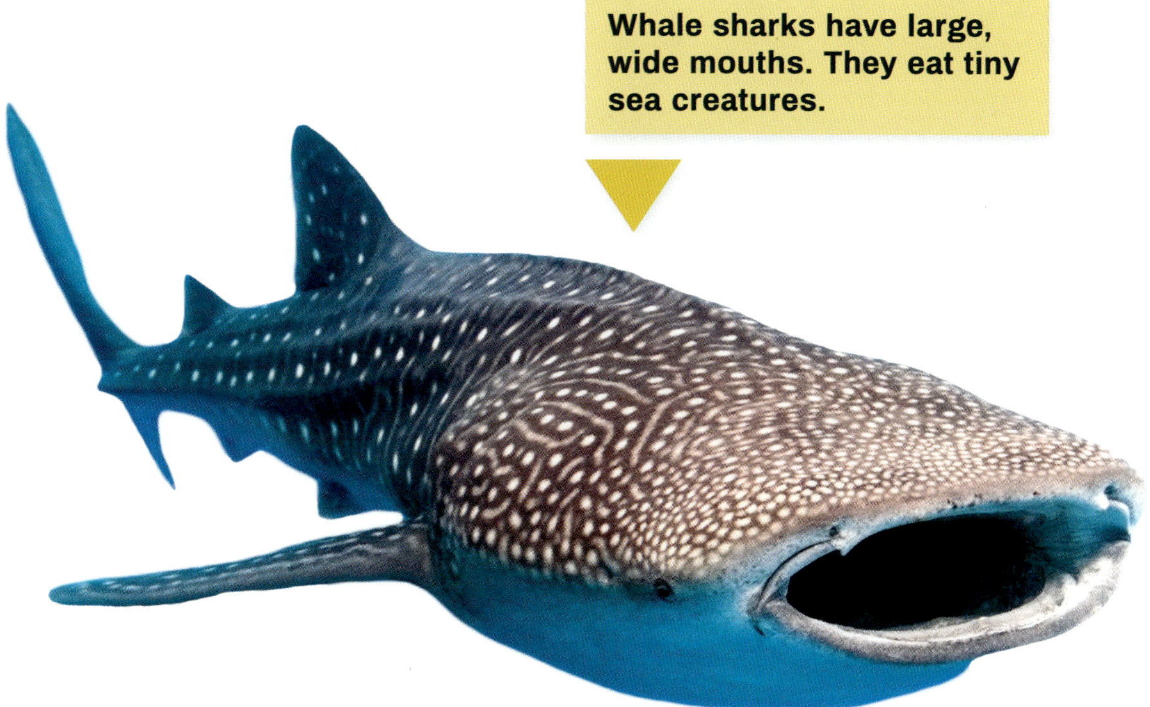

Visitors can see a giant squid at the Natural History Museum in London.

Some squid are very big, too. One giant squid measured nearly 43 feet (13 m) long. That is longer than a school bus.

FAST FACT
Giant squid have the largest eyes of any animal. Each eye is about the size of a soccer ball.

CHAPTER 3

BIGGEST ON LAND

The largest land animal is the African elephant. These elephants weigh about 18,000 pounds (8,000 kg). And they can stand 13 feet (4 m) tall.

African elephants can live for as long as 70 years.

The giraffe is the tallest animal. It can grow 19 feet (6 m) tall.

A giraffe's long neck helps it eat leaves off trees.

Ostriches can't fly. But they can run up to 43 miles per hour (70 km/h).

BIGGEST BIRD

The ostrich is the largest and tallest bird. It stands 9 feet (3 m) tall. And it can weigh more than 300 pounds (140 kg).

Saltwater crocodiles are the largest **reptiles**. Males can reach lengths of 23 feet (7 m). And they can weigh more than 2,200 pounds (1,000 kg).

Some saltwater crocodiles are big enough to catch and eat wild buffalo.

Adult capybaras are about 4 feet (1.2 m) long.

FAST FACT

Capybaras are the biggest **rodents**. Adults can weigh 174 pounds (79 kg).

CHAPTER 4

The great bustard is the heaviest animal that can fly. This bird can weigh 40 pounds (18 kg) or more.

Great bustards live in dry, grassy areas.

Albatrosses use their long wings to soar. They can fly many miles without flapping much.

The wandering albatross has the biggest **wingspan**. Its wings can stretch 12.1 feet (3.7 m) across. The great white pelican comes in second. Its wingspan is 11.8 feet (3.6 m).

FAST FACT

A wandering albatross can fly 10,000 miles (16,000 km) without stopping.

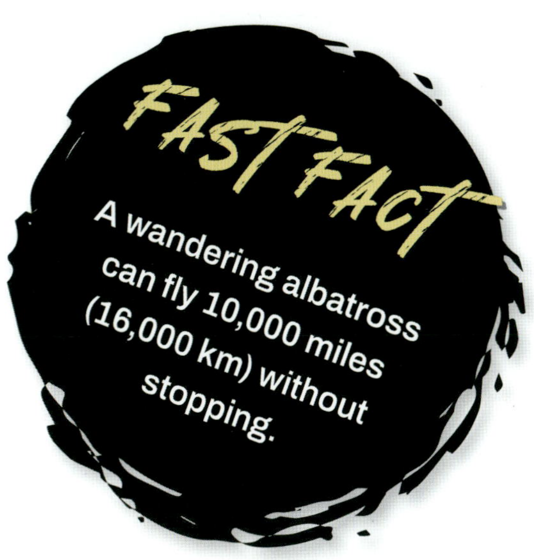

Great white pelicans have long wings and huge beaks.

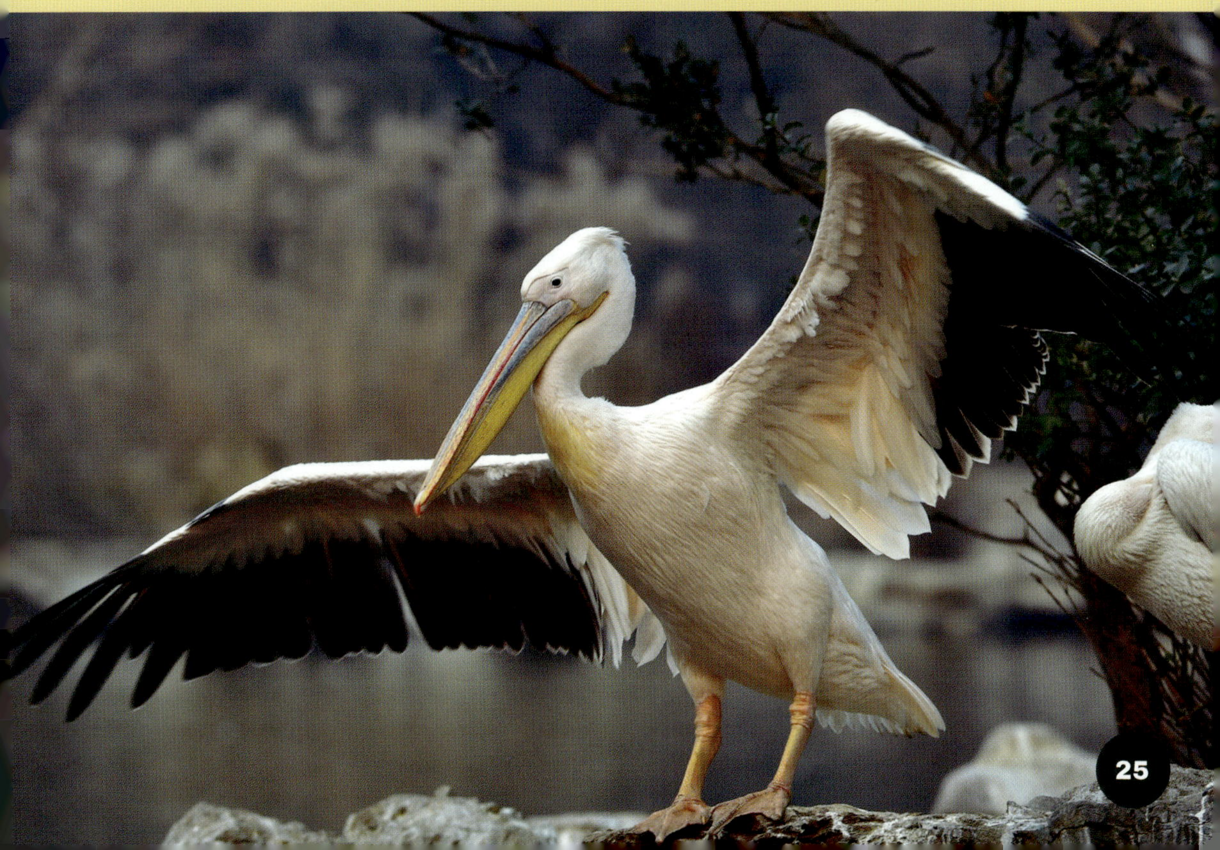

Flying fox bats often hang upside down from trees.

The golden-crowned flying fox is the world's biggest bat. It is also the largest flying **mammal**. Its wings can be 5.5 feet (1.7 m) across.

FLYING REPTILES

Long ago, Earth had even bigger flying animals. They were reptiles called pterosaurs. Some had wingspans of 40 feet (12 m). Scientists learned about them by studying **fossils**.

Most fossils of pterosaurs show just the bones.

COMPREHENSION QUESTIONS

Write your answers on a separate piece of paper.

1. Write a few sentences describing the largest animal on land.

2. Which animal's size do you think is most impressive? Why?

3. What is the largest animal that lives in the water?

A. whale shark
B. blue whale
C. fin whale

4. Which of the following animals has the longest body?

A. giant squid
B. whale shark
C. saltwater crocodile

5. What does **measured** mean in this book?

*Some squid are very big, too. One giant squid **measured** nearly 43 feet (13 m) long.*

- **A.** used a ruler
- **B.** took a picture
- **C.** was a certain size

6. What does **creature** mean in this book?

*The lion's mane jellyfish is the longest sea **creature**.*

- **A.** a monster
- **B.** an animal
- **C.** a plant

Answer key on page 32.

GLOSSARY

blowhole

A hole at the top of a whale's head that is used for breathing.

calf

A baby whale.

fossils

Remains of plants and animals that lived long ago.

mammal

An animal that has hair and produces milk for its young.

massive

Very large.

reptiles

Cold-blooded animals that have scales.

rodents

Small, furry animals with large front teeth, such as rats or mice.

tentacles

The flexible limbs of animals such as squid or jellyfish.

wingspan

The length from the tip of one wing to the other.

BOOKS

Brundle, Joanna. *The Scale of Animals*. New York: Crabtree Publishing, 2020.

Jackson, Tom. *World's Biggest Reptiles*. Minneapolis: Lerner Publishing, 2019.

Schuh, Mari. *Blue Whales.* North Mankato, MN: Capstone Publishing, 2020.

ONLINE RESOURCES

Visit **www.apexeditions.com** to find links and resources related to this title.

ABOUT THE AUTHOR

Marissa Kirkman is a writer and editor who lives in Illinois. She enjoys reading about animals, science, and history.

INDEX

ANSWER KEY:
1. Answers will vary; 2. Answers will vary; 3. B; 4. A; 5. C; 6. B

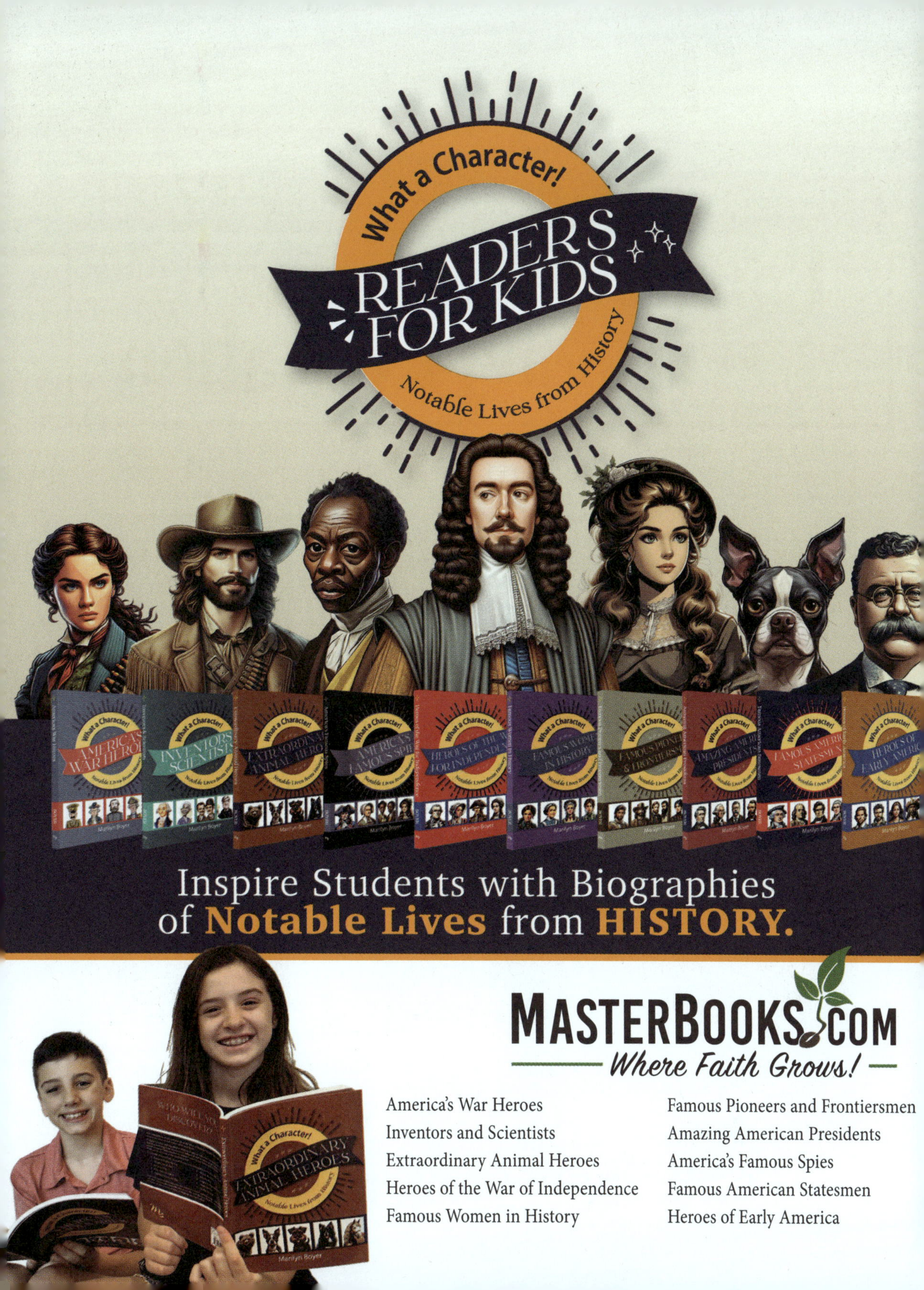
What a Character!
READERS FOR KIDS
Notable Lives from History
Inspire Students with Biographies of Notable Lives from HISTORY.
MASTERBOOKS.COM
Where Faith Grows!
America's War Heroes
Inventors and Scientists
Extraordinary Animal Heroes
Heroes of the War of Independence
Famous Women in History
Famous Pioneers and Frontiersmen
Amazing American Presidents
America's Famous Spies
Famous American Statesmen
Heroes of Early America

Language Lessons for a Living Education

GRADE 1
LANGUAGE LESSONS FOR A LIVING EDUCATION 1
978-1-68344-211-0

GRADE 2
LANGUAGE LESSONS FOR A LIVING EDUCATION 2
978-1-68344-122-9

GRADE 3
LANGUAGE LESSONS FOR A LIVING EDUCATION 3
978-1-68344-137-3

GRADE 4
LANGUAGE LESSONS FOR A LIVING EDUCATION 4
978-1-68344-138-0

GRADE 5
LANGUAGE LESSONS FOR A LIVING EDUCATION 5
978-1-68344-178-6

GRADE 6
LANGUAGE LESSONS FOR A LIVING EDUCATION 6
978-1-68344-209-7

VISIT MASTERBOOKS.COM TO SEE OUR FULL LINE OF FAITH-BUILDING CURRICULUM
Where Faith Grows!

First printing: April 2024
Third printing: May 2026

Master Books, P.O. Box 726, Green Forest, AR 72638

Master Books® is a division of the New Leaf Publishing Group, LLC.

ISBN: 978-1-68344-365-0
ISBN: 978-1-61458-880-1 (digital)
Library of Congress Control Number: 2024934948

Cover: Diana Bogardus
Interior: Terry White

Please consider requesting that a copy of this volume be purchased by your local library system.

Printed in the United States of America

Please visit our website for other great titles:
www.masterbooks.com

For information regarding promotional opportunities,
please contact the publicity department at pr@nlpg.com.

Table of Contents

Image Credits

Interior images were art-directed and refined by the Master Books design team, using Shutterstock AI as a production tool.

1

Sybil Ludington – Brave Messenger

April 26, 1777	Near Danbury, Connecticut

It was during the War of Independence that the British forces landed on April 25, 1777, at the mouth of the Saugatuck River with plans to attack Danbury, Connecticut. Danbury was only 25 miles from Long Island Sound. Major General William Tryon, royal governor of New York, had orders from General William Howe to destroy the Continental Army's military supplies stored there.

Who Was Sybil Ludington?

Sybil Ludington, the eldest of 12 children, was born on April 5, 1761, in Frederick (now Ludingtonville), New York. The family lived on a farm of over 200 acres. Her father was Colonel Henry Ludington. He had served under General William Tryon during the French and Indian War when he was fighting with the British. Now, he was on the side of the Americans fighting for independence from the harsh rule of King George III.

At the start of the Revolution, Colonel Ludington served as **aide-de-camp** to General George Washington. Since he had military experience, the local militia made him colonel of a unit of 400 men in Western New York. His job was to organize and train the militiamen in case they were needed to **repel** British attacks. The British offered a

aide-de-camp: Confidential assistant

repel: Oppose

reward for the capture of Sybil's father, so the family had to constantly be on guard. Sybil, though only 16 years old, often acted as a kind of **sentinel**, looking out for the family's welfare. The Ludington family's farmland was a **strategic** point between Connecticut and Long Island, which made the **Tories** want to **confiscate** it for their own use.

Always on Guard

One night, Sybil and her youngest sister Rebecca were standing guard when they saw a group of Tories surrounding their house. They quickly called to their four brothers and two sisters, gave them candles, and had them walk back and forth in front of the windows in every room of the house. The moving **silhouettes** in the candlelight created the impression that the house was heavily guarded. It worked! The Tories decided against attacking. Sybil and her siblings had tricked the Tories and escaped danger this time.

sentinel: Guard

strategic: Having a military advantage

Tories: Those loyal to the king

confiscate: Take possession of

silhouette: an outline against a lighter background

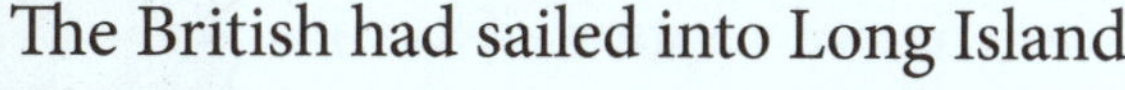

The British had sailed into Long Island Sound with 20 transports and six warships. There were 2,000 British troops aboard. They anchored in the mouth of the Saugatuck River, which was just 30 miles from the Ludington's home. They intended to destroy the supplies the Continentals had stored in Danbury. The supplies were crucial for the survival of the Continental Army. They included 5,000 pairs of badly needed shoes, socks, a printing press, bedding for army hospitals, thousands of bushels of grain, barrels of molasses, hundreds of barrels of beef and pork, and more than 1,000 tents, as well as muskets and ammunition.

As the British made their way toward Danbury, colonists hearing they were approaching began fleeing town. Some were taking wagons filled with their belongings over the badly rutted roads. Some were hiding in the woods or barns. Some were concealing their horses and livestock in the forests. Only a few decided to stay to guard their homes. Normally, 50 Continental soldiers guarded the town, but they were away fighting. The militia consisted of only 100 men. They were not enough to stand up against thousands of British soldiers. Danbury needed to be defended or all would be lost!

The British Descend on Danbury

Governor Tryon confiscated a house to set up his headquarters — the home of Nehemiah Dibble. Other British generals were **surveying** the town searching for suitable lodgings. Four young men were hiding in a house and fired at the British troops. The house was immediately set on fire, killing the men. The British were to be feared. Terrified, the families still in town tried to hide. One building that contained grain was burned to the ground. Another that held barrels of meat was burned, and fat from the meat ran in a stream down the street. To complicate matters, a rainstorm was brewing, threatening to turn the roads into a muddy mess.

surveying: Looking over

Around 9 p.m., the Ludingtons, unaware of what was happening in Danbury, heard a rider gallop up to the house. He breathlessly announced that Colonel Ludington was to **muster** his militia and set out to defend Danbury. There was one problem, though. Ludington's men had been allowed to return to their homes to plant their spring crops. Their farms were scattered far and wide throughout the countryside. It would take hours to alert them. And who could he send? The messenger who had arrived at his house was exhausted from his long, hard ride. Colonel Ludington himself needed to

muster: Gather

be available to lead his troops when they arrived. There was no time to waste.

A book written in 1907 featuring some of Colonel Ludington's memoirs states, "In this emergency, he turned to his daughter, Sybil, who a few days before, had passed her 16th birthday, and bade her to take a horse, ride for the men, and tell them to be at his house by daybreak."[1]

Sybil had a trusted horse named Star that she had trained herself. Her father had given Star to her when he had observed her love for and skill with horses. Sybil would ride each day after her chores were done. She was an expert rider and was known by all in the region. Her father trained the militia at their farm, and Sybil had grown up helping him by running errands and acting as a messenger for the militia. She knew where each militia man lived.

Sybil's Ride

It was a 40-mile ride and a dangerous mission. Bands of thieves known as "cowboys and skinners" often hid in the forest waiting to steal from those who might be passing by. To add to the danger, rain began to beat down on Sybil. She rode along the Croton River as she pressed forward to the town of Carmel. Arriving there, she shouted out loudly, "The British are burning Danbury! Tell the militia to join my father

at Ludington's mill. Tell your neighbors!"[2] She continued to alert the country folk by banging on their doors with a heavy stick. Sybil forged ahead to Kent Fields and then Redding Corners and finally back to Frederick, braving the driving rain as she raced through the countryside. Men were quick to volunteer and heed Sybil's warning. Soon, militiamen assembled at Ludington's mill. The march of ten miles to Danbury was made by many men that night.

Meanwhile, the British were proceeding to destroy Danbury. They found a supply of liquor and began to drink it. That **diversion** distracted the soldiers and slowed down the destruction, allowing a bit more time for the militia to gather. When General Tryon got the news that some of the Patriots were only a few miles away, he sent an order to rouse his sleeping men. Then he gave the order to destroy their foes. Houses marked with a cross belonged to Tories, and they were to leave those houses alone. Nineteen homes and stores were soon in flames.

diversion: Turning aside from an intended purpose

Tryon Retreats

General Tryon knew he needed to retreat before the Continental reinforcements showed up. He began to head his men back to their ships, but on

the way, he wanted to leave Danbury in flames. He suspected American troops would be waiting for him on the road by which he'd come into town. With the help of some Tories, he found another road for his retreat. Patriot citizens burned bridges and did all they could to deter his progress. American generals split their forces.

Tryon and his troops were busy eating breakfast when American General David Wooster's troops came upon them. The Battle of Ridgefield was the result. During the fighting, General Wooster was struck in the back of his head with a musket ball and died. Ludington's troops pursued the British as they retreated. An article in the *Connecticut Journal* reported, "The enemy's loss is judged to be more than double our numbers, and about twenty prisoners."[3] **Skirmishes** continued to be fought all along the way until the British finally boarded their ships. By this time, Sybil was likely fast asleep in her own bed after her exhausting but successful night's work. Sybil had saved the day!

skirmishes: Small battles

Sybil Is Praised

Tryon's men reported 50 to 60 enlisted men and five officers killed or wounded in the two-hour Battle of Ridgefield alone. The British never again dared to attack the Connecticut interior. In the book *Colonel Henry Ludington: A Memoir*, this tribute is given:

> "There is no extravagance in comparing her ride with that of Paul Revere and its midnight message. Nor was her errand less efficient than his."[4]

Comparing Sybil's ride to Paul Revere, she rode twice as far, through dirt roads, in the dark of night, and through driving rain. Unlike Paul Revere, Sybil was able to avoid being captured. Paul Revere also had help from William Dawes and Wentworth Cheswell, who were also spreading the word that the British were coming. Sybil made the ride all by herself.

In 1935, the New York State Education Department placed a series of roadside signs marking the route Sybil and her faithful horse Star took that night. In 1961, a sculptor named Anna Hyatt Huntington molded a statue of Sybil, the ardent Patriot girl on her faithful horse, spreading her cry of alarm. The original statue is in the

town of Carmel and a smaller one is in Danbury. The Daughters of the American Revolution Museum in Washington, D.C., also has a smaller statue. A picture of Sybil was put on a postage stamp in 1975 as part of the **Bicentennial** Series.

After the War

Sybil continued to live with her parents until she married Edmond Ogden when she was 23. The couple gave birth to one son, Henry, born in 1786. Henry was only 13 when his father died of yellow fever, a highly contagious and deadly disease at the time. Sybil bought and ran a **tavern** in Catskill, New York, to support herself and Henry. When she sold it six years later, she made a profit of three times the purchase price. With that money, she bought Henry, who now had a new wife, a home in Unadilla, New York. She lived there with them for the next 30 years and enjoyed being a grandmother to their four sons and two daughters. Sybil died on February 26, 1839, at age 77 and was buried next to her parents in Patterson, New York. There have been several poems written about Sybil Ludington's famous ride, which can be found in books and other historical resources.

Bicentennial: 200th birthday

tavern: Restaurant and meeting place

2

Abigail Adams – John's Dearest Friend

1744–1818	Boston, Massachusetts Area

Who Was Abigail Adams?

Abigail Smith was born on November 11, 1744, on a farm near Boston, Massachusetts. Abigail's mother taught her to read and to do arithmetic. Her father was minister of North Parish Church in Weymouth, a town 13 miles south of Boston. He had an extensive library in his home with hundreds of books, and he encouraged Abigail to read them. She studied the Bible and classic literature, memorized poems, and read books on many topics. Her father encouraged her to listen when visitors came to talk about the troubles with Great Britain. Abigail was very interested in politics and had strong opinions.

Meeting John Adams

One visitor who sometimes came to the Smith home was John Adams. He was a 24-year-old lawyer when he first met 15-year-old Abigail. Both agreed on many issues and loved politics. They developed a friendship that ended up in marriage five years later. John's father gave them a 100-year-old home in nearby Braintree. John was a lawyer, but he loved farming, too, and Abigail loved being a farmwife. She cooked, churned her own

butter, collected the eggs, preserved food from her garden for the winter, and cared for their sheep, cows, and chickens. A little over nine months after their marriage, they had a baby girl. They named her Abigail but called her "Nabby."

When the British Parliament passed the **Stamp Act** in 1765, John began writing opinion articles in the *Boston Gazette* (a weekly newspaper in Boston). After the birth of their first son, John Quincy, they decided to move to Boston so John could be closer to his work. There he joined the Sons of Liberty, a group of Patriots who opposed the **tyranny** of King George III. John and Abigail were hospitable and used their home to entertain many key Patriots such as Sam Adams, John Hancock, Josiah Quincy, and Joseph Warren. Abigail's sister lived in Boston and so did her dear friend, Mercy Warren. Abigail missed the farm but loved entertaining friends.

Stamp Act: Tax on documents

tyranny: Oppressive control

Abigail loved writing letters from the time she was a young girl. She wrote over 3,000 letters in her lifetime! John had to be away from

home often, so she and John **corresponded** often during the War of Independence. Many of those letters were compiled into a book that is still in print today. They offer much information about what it was like to live during those times. By 1772, Abigail and John had six children.

corresponded: Wrote letters

Tax on Tea

When tensions built over the British tax on tea, Abigail, along with most Patriot women, stopped drinking British tea and creatively made her own from berry leaves. They called it "Liberty Tea." John and Abigail supported the Boston Tea Party when Patriots dumped the chests of tea into Boston Harbor in protest of the imposed tax. They both felt strongly that Americans needed to secure their freedom and were willing to sacrifice to obtain it.

John was elected to go to the First Continental Congress in Philadelphia on behalf of Massachusetts. Abigail wanted him to go, but this left her alone to run the household. She resorted to letter-writing to keep in touch with her

beloved husband. She kept him informed about what was happening in Boston. She always addressed John as 'Dearest Friend' when writing to him. They both felt war was **inevitable**. Abigail reported to John about the conditions in the camps, health of the soldiers, local politics, and reputations of the British generals living in Boston. She told him of the troubles citizens faced when the British came and took over their homes. She reported that food was scarce and many folks were leaving the city.

War Comes

When war broke out at Lexington, John feared for his family's safety. He wrote to Abigail, "In case of real danger ... fly to the woods with our children."[5] Abigail opened her home to people fleeing Boston and to Patriot soldiers coming into the city. Her house was full of friends and strangers, and Abigail somehow managed to feed them all. People slept in every part of the house, including the attic and even in the barn. Abigail was constantly kept busy supplying the things they normally would have bought from England. She had to make their

inevitable: Sure to come

own soap and spin her own cloth. Using ashes from fires and also juice of berries, she made ink. Abigail even melted down **pewter** spoons to make bullets for the soldiers. When money was running low, Abigail asked John to send her 6,000 sewing pins so that she might sell them and bring in some money. Her passion for freedom kept her going.

pewter: Mixture of tin and copper

Sickness Strikes

In the summer of 1775, there was an outbreak of dysentery. It is a sickness from contaminated food that causes intestinal upset. Eight of Abigail's neighbors died in one week! John's brother was one of those who died. Abigail herself got dysentery but recovered. When their youngest son Thomas got ill, Abigail's mother came to help nurse him; sadly, her mother got sick and died. It was so difficult for Abigail, having John gone and bearing all the hardships alone! The winter started out to be a very cold one. John came home briefly at Christmas, but Abigail knew he must return to the Continental Congress. Liberty was at stake and his country needed him.

The British Leave Boston

On June 17, 1775, Abigail and the children awoke to the sound of the thunder of cannons. A messenger came to the door announcing that the Patriots were trying to hold Bunker Hill in Charlestown, just across the river. Abigail and seven-year-old John Quincy climbed to the top of the hill on their property and stood looking across the harbor at the flashes from cannon fire.

Abigail, writing a letter to John, said, "The race is not to the swift, nor the battle to the strong; but the God of Israel is he, that giveth strength and power unto His people. Trust in Him at all times, ye people, pour out your hearts before Him; God is a refuge for us. Charlestown is laid in ashes. The battle began upon our entrenchments upon Bunker's Hill, Saturday morning about three o'clock, and has not ceased yet, and it is now three o'clock Sabbath afternoon. It is expected they will come over the Neck tonight, and a dreadful battle must ensue. Almighty God, cover the heads of our countrymen, and be a shield to our dear friends."[6]

The Americans lost the battle, but only because they had run out of ammunition. Although the British won, they realized it had been too costly in the loss of men. The British suffered twice as many wounded and killed as the Patriots and lost many officers as well. John and Abigail mourned the loss of their dear friend Dr. Joseph Warren, who fell in battle.

Dorchester Heights

In March 1776, the Patriot soldiers succeeded in working all through the night to build fortifications on Dorchester Heights that overlooked the town of Boston. More than 1,200 soldiers and volunteers and 300 oxcarts transported tools and materials to the site as quietly as possible. In the morning, the British were astonished to discover the newly erected defenses. Abigail later wrote to John, telling him British General William Howe had commented on the fortifications built by the Americans. "These fellows have done more work in one night than I could make my army do in three months."[7]

General Washington, aided by a fierce, violent thunderstorm, succeeded in driving the British from Boston without firing a single shot. Abigail wrote to John, "It's time we cut all our ties to England. I long to hear Congress has declared independence."[8] She didn't have long to wait. In July, the Declaration of Independence was adopted. Church bells rang and people rejoiced in the streets as the Declaration of Independence was read aloud. Abigail gathered her children in the house that evening and together they prayed, thanking God and asking for His guidance for the new nation. Independence had been declared, but there was still much hardship ahead.

John Goes to Paris

John returned home from the Continental Congress after being gone for a year. Unfortunately, he had to leave a few months later for Paris to try to get the French to help the American cause. He took their ten-year-old son John Quincy with him. Abigail wrote this advice to her son:

> "**Adhere** to those religious sentiments and principles which were early instilled into your mind and remember that you are accountable to your Maker for all your words and actions...."[9]

adhere: Hold fast

Again, Abigail was left to run the family farm and care for the children. John and John Quincy ran into a bit of trouble. First, the British attacked their ship, then they managed to escape pirates, and finally, they survived a terrible storm that lasted for three days. One of the crew was killed by lightning. Abigail was worried. She didn't hear from them for months. There had been a rumor that their ship had been captured by the British, so she was greatly relieved when a letter finally arrived confirming their safe arrival.

Winter was hard for Abigail with John gone. There were many bad snowstorms in Braintree, and the farm wasn't doing well financially.

Abigail thought of a plan. She asked John to send her items she could resell, such as cloth, dishes, and ribbons. Abigail was good with business. She began ordering items directly from trading houses in Europe and soon was making a profit. She then invested her profits in land and bonds; years later, the money was still providing for their needs.

After a year and a half, John and John Quincy finally came home. Abigail hadn't heard they were coming; it was a total and wonderful surprise when they knocked on her door. The following November, John had to leave again. This time he took not only John Quincy but their son Charles as well. Although Abigail hated to see them go, she felt the boys needed to be with their father. This time, it was almost five years before she saw her husband and sons again as they were traveling overseas. What huge personal sacrifices this woman made to see liberty obtained!

The War Ends

Finally, in 1783, the War of Independence came to an end. The United States was now an independent nation. However, many decisions were

still necessary to **establish** this new nation. John remained in France helping to write peace **treaties** that would allow the United States to do business with other countries. John wrote to Abigail, "It's my duty to help our new nation grow great and powerful. Yet, I cannot live here any longer without you. Will you come?"[10]

establish: Create a government for

treaties: Agreements between countries

They decided that Abigail should sail for London to be with John at last. Nabby traveled with her. The other children would stay with their Aunt Elizabeth. Elizabeth's husband, a minister, would prepare them to enter Harvard College when old enough. The voyage was very difficult. Both Abigail and Nabby were seasick most of the way. John Quincy met them when they arrived. He was now quite grown up, 17 years old. All four then traveled to Paris where John had rented a beautiful house. Abigail and Nabby attended many fancy parties with Benjamin Franklin and Thomas Jefferson. John continued to work making treaties while John Quincy acted as his secretary. Abigail wrote to her sisters, "I see plays and **operas** in Paris and I like them but my heart keeps returning to my own home."[11]

operas: Classical music performances

Congress appointed John Adams to be the first American Ambassador to England. John Quincy decided it was time to return home and enroll in Harvard. John and Abigail left for London. They moved into a large house on Grosvenor Square. Abigail hired a maid, a **butler**, a cook, and a **coachman**. Nabby met and married Colonel William Smith, secretary in the American Embassy, and in a year had a baby. John and Abigail were now proud grandparents. Three years later, John's term as Ambassador was finished and John and Abigail could finally return to America. Abigail couldn't wait to see her sons. She wanted to be home at last.

butler: Male servant to oversee the household

coachman: Driver of a horse-drawn carriage

Back Home

John Quincy was studying law. He had graduated from Harvard with honors. Charles and Tommy were still attending school there. John and Abigail bought a house in Quincy, south of Boston, and bought cows, sheep, and pigs. However, they didn't stay on their farm for long. In the spring, John was elected Vice-President of the United States. It was a great honor. The capital then was in New York. Abigail stayed behind for a while to sell all their animals. It was June before she reached the

comfortable house John had rented for them in New York. Abigail gave many pleasant parties for members of Congress and their wives.

President Washington appointed 26-year-old John Quincy as Minister to Holland. Thomas acted as his secretary. Abigail was pleased. "It's one of my chief blessings to have sons worthy of the trust of our country. Serve it with honor as your father does."[12]

President

John was elected President of the United States in 1797. Abigail was not present when he was sworn in, as she was tending to John's 89-year-old mother who died in her arms. When Abigail joined him, she began to give dinner parties, write letters, of course, organize the servants, and plan for each day. To get it all done, she would get up at 5:00 a.m. every day. She was very aware of what was happening in politics and would talk over the issues with John. He was thankful for her input. She was so involved that people began to call her "Mrs. President."

When John's term as President ended, Abigail and John finally got to their farm and enjoyed being with family and each other. They had spent so many years apart while John was serving his country and helping to fight for freedom. Now they were surrounded by grandchildren. In 1814, John and Abigail celebrated their 50th wedding anniversary. Abigail said, "I have great cause for thankfulness."[13]

In October 1818, Abigail came down with **typhoid fever**. She told John when she was no longer useful, she was ready to go to heaven. She died on October 28 at the age of 73. John wished he could die with her, his dearest friend, but he lived eight more years. Six years after Abigail's death, John Quincy became the sixth President of the United States. Abigail had been the wife of one President and mother of another. She had sacrificed so much time with her beloved John for the sake of her country and left a **legacy** of inspiration to us all.

typhoid fever: Life-threatening bacterial infection

legacy: Long-lasting impact

Deborah Sampson – The Soldier with a Secret

May 1782–October 1783	West Point, New York

The Battle of Yorktown had already taken place. The War for American Independence was drawing to a close but was certainly not over. **Recruits** were still needed to handle the many conflicts that continued between the Patriots and British, aided by their Tory helpers. Groups loyal to the British Crown would lead attacks on civilians and Patriot soldiers. Skirmishes continued for two years until the peace treaty was formally signed and the war officially ended.

Who Was Deborah Sampson?

Deborah Sampson was born on a farm in Plymouth, Massachusetts, on December 17, 1760. Her parents struggled to make a living. When Deborah was only five years old, her father, a sailor, was shipwrecked and lost at sea. Her mother, **destitute**, was forced to find homes for her children with relatives or friends who were able to care for them. Deborah went to live with her mother's cousin, Miss Fuller, who treated her as if she were her own child. Deborah learned many household skills, but she especially learned to love reading at an early age. Life was wonderful for three years, but then Cousin Fuller died.

recruits: New soldiers

destitute: Without money

Off to Work

After that, the only person her mother could find to take Deborah was an 80-year-old lady named Mrs. Thatcher, who lived in Middleborough, Massachusetts. Mrs. Thatcher was **feeble** and unable to do any chores. Although Deborah was only eight years old, she had all the work to do: carrying heavy wood, cooking, laundry, and even spoon-feeding Mrs. Thatcher. It was a pretty miserable existence. A minister from Middleborough would come by to check on Deborah. He decided to try to find a way to get the girl out of that situation. Old Mrs. Thatcher went to live with relatives; Deborah went to live with Deacon Thomas's family in Middleborough.

feeble: Weak and sickly

At last, Deborah was living with a family again but, of course, it was not quite the same as her own. Here, she was a household servant and would have to work for ten years to pay for her room, board, clothes, and food. This was common for many poor families during this time. Fortunately, she did have her own little room in the **loft**. Deborah was kept busy caring for the household and four lively little boys as well.

There wasn't much time left for reading, which is what she loved to do. In addition to all her heavy farming chores, Deborah taught the boys how to read. When it came time for the boys to attend school, Deborah would borrow their schoolbooks and read every night by candlelight. She taught herself to

loft: Space under the roof

write as well. Deacon Thomas wanted all children to learn how to handle money, so he allowed Deborah to care for and sell some lambs and keep the money she earned from the sales. She saved her money. The Thomas boys grew, and the oldest went off to fight in the American War for Independence.

Free At Last

Deborah at last turned 18. Her ten years were up, and she was free to leave the Thomas's home. She was asked to be the village schoolteacher since most of the men had gone off to fight in the war. She taught for a while. She also supported herself by working at different farms in the area. All this time, she was saving up her money. Deborah watched the soldiers drilling and marching off to the army. She wished she could serve her country in some way, too. Then she came up with a secret plan. Why not? She would cut her hair and take some of her savings to buy some men's clothing. She would present herself as a soldier. She walked miles away from home so she would not be recognized. Signing up to be a Continental soldier was a three-year commitment.

On May 23, 1782, Deborah Sampson signed up for the 4th Massachusetts Regiment. She signed her name as "Robert Shurtliff."

Her uniform did not fit her well, so she made **alterations**. When asked by the men how she knew how to sew, she explained that she had once been **apprenticed** to a **tailor**.

Her first assignment was to West Point, a fort north of New York City, where she would be in the light infantry. The light infantry consisted of soldiers who marched before the main army. She was one of the 10,000 soldiers drilling daily, learning to march in formation, use a **bayonet**, and load and shoot a musket twice in one minute. Deborah wrote to her mother so she wouldn't worry, explaining she had found employment in a "large, but well-regulated family. I shall endeavor to make that prudence my model for which I own am indebted to those who took charge of my youth. Heaven grant that a speedy and lasting peace may constitute us a happy and independent nation that I may once more return to the embraces of a parent whom I love."[14]

alterations: Adjustments by sewing

apprenticed: Taught the trade by working

tailor: One who makes clothes

bayonet: Blade attached to a rifle

Life in Disguise

"Robert" was teased at times for not growing a mustache or beard, but many of the boys in the army were so young that was not unusual. The men called her "Bobby." Robert went out with men on **scouting** and **raiding** missions and always performed "his" duties with honor and skill. Deborah had worked hard all her life, but the army was still a challenge. She had to march

scouting: Exploring to gain information

raiding: Surprise attack

long distances, her shoes fell apart, and she got blisters and sores on her hands and feet, but she never complained. Neither did she participate when the men would drink or wrestle together. She stayed by herself as much as possible, although she was friendly to all. Everyone liked her.

In the summer of 1782, while **patrolling** an area around Tarrytown, New York, Deborah's unit was attacked by a group of Tories with bayonets. Deborah received a deep cut on the leg from a bayonet and was also shot twice in the thigh. She was carried to a field hospital. The surgeon, distracted by the large number of patients, treated a wound Deborah had received on the head and asked if that was all. She nodded because she didn't want to be **detected** as being a woman in **disguise**.

She used her pocketknife to try to remove the bullet in her leg. She was able to remove one musket ball. There was still one buried deep into her leg. The pain was more than she could bear when she tried to dig deeper to reach it. That bullet remained with her for life, often causing her pain. Deborah bandaged her leg, left the hospital, and made her way back to camp.

Robert Shurtliff's qualities caught the attention of General John Paterson, who made the young soldier his **orderly**. Soon General Paterson was treating Robert more like an equal because of his diligence and ability. When General Paterson was sent to Philadelphia, his orderly accompanied him.

patrolling: Guarding

detected: Discovered

disguise: Concealing one's identity

orderly: enlisted officer who serves an officer

Epidemic

While in Philadelphia, an **epidemic** was raging among the troops. "Shurtliff" became ill with a fever and was taken to a hospital **delirious**. The doctor, Dr. Binney, realized his patient was not a boy. He called for the hospital **matron**, told her the secret, and had Deborah transferred to the matron's quarters to continue her recovery. As Deborah began to improve, Dr. Binney introduced her to his wife and family as "Robert Shurtliff," and praised the brave soldier. Deborah took walks with the Binney family through parks and gardens. She was invited to some fine houses in Philadelphia, always introduced as a Continental soldier.

epidemic: Extremely contagious sickness

delirious: Unaware of what was happening due to the fever

matron: Woman supervisor

No one else was told about her disguise until Deborah had fully recovered and returned to General Paterson. Deborah was afraid she might get in trouble, but the general said, "You have nothing to fear … You have only my admiration and respect."[15] The general sent "Robert" to General Washington, bearing a letter of explanation. After thoughtfully reading

the letter, General Washington thanked her for her service, gave her an honorable discharge, and kindly gave her some money for her journey home. The war had ended, and so had Deborah's life in the army.

Home Again

For a while, Deborah lived with her mother and returned to farm work. She immediately began wearing dresses again. Her disguise had only been to serve her country. She would wear a uniform again for certain Veterans' Day parades, but she was evermore a lady. After the war, President Washington invited Deborah Sampson to visit him. He told how bravely she had fought for the new nation. Congress presented her with a land grant and a soldier's pension, which was half-pay for life to soldiers disabled in the service and unable to earn a living.

Deborah Marries

A few years later, Deborah met and married Benjamin Gannett, a hardworking farmer from Sharon, Massachusetts. Benjamin and Deborah had three children, two daughters and a son who, one day, would become a soldier. Deborah also took in and raised a baby,

Susanna, whose mother had died. Deborah was a gentle mother. She had seen enough of fighting. She taught her children to be peaceful and kind to others. The family always had to struggle to make a living. Deborah's wound, as well as exposure to the weather and conditions during the war, affected her health. She could no longer do heavy work around the farm.

When she was in her 40s, Deborah made a few appearances before audiences, describing her experiences in the war. She would begin her performance with her dress on but end by wearing a military uniform. She marched, performed drills with her musket, and told some details about her hidden life as "Robert Shurtliff." She did not do it for fame but to bring in some extra money. She would close her performance by singing "God Save the Sixteen States."

In the early 1800s, Deborah met Paul Revere. When he heard her story, he offered to try to get her another pension from the United States Congress for her service. He wrote a letter to recommend her, describing Deborah as "a woman of handsome talents, good morals, a cheerful wife, and an affectionate parent. She is now much out of health."[16] He attributed her poor health to her war service and the bullet still in her leg. He ended his letter by appealing, "I have no

doubt your humanity will prompt you to do all in your power to get her some relief, I think her case much more deserving than hundreds to whom Congress has been generous."[17] Revere's letter resulted in an additional pension for Deborah. She was given $8 a month until she died on April 29, 1827, at the age of 67.

Deborah has been remembered for her service. In 1944, during World War II, a Liberty ship was named after her — the *Deborah Gannett*. A street in Sharon, Massachusetts, near the house where she lived with Ben and her children, is named Deborah Sampson Street. Deborah was the only woman to earn a full military pension for participation in the Revolutionary Army.

4

Dolley Madison – Saving George Washington

War of 1812	Washington, D.C.

America won her independence in 1776, but troubles with England began to **escalate** again. The fighting at first was at sea when the British attempted to restrict U.S. trade. Their navy was always short of volunteers, so they resorted to hiring gangs to force American seamen to serve in the British military against their will. Almost half of all seamen in the Royal Navy were **impressed** this way. America's efforts to expand her borders to the Great Lakes met with stubborn British resistance. The British enlisted Native Americans to help them fight. In August of 1814, the British set out to capture and burn Washington, D.C., the nation's new capital city.

escalate: Grow

impressed: Forced to serve

Who Was Dolley Madison?

John Payne was a Virginia plantation owner and a Quaker. Quakers believed slavery was wrong, but for years British rule and then Virginia law had prevented a person from selling slaves he had inherited even if he wanted to. When that law changed, John Payne was one of the first Quakers to sell his plantation at Scotchtown, Virginia. He freed his beloved slaves and moved his family from Virginia to Philadelphia. It was a brave but necessary move. It was impossible

to run a plantation without the slaves to help with crops, horses, brickmaking, meat **curing**, and the many other jobs involved in running a plantation. John was sure he was making the right choice. He would sell his land and buildings and use that money to start a business to support his wife and eight children.

He decided to open a store in Philadelphia. His daughter, Dolley, was 15 years old at the time. She was torn about the move. She loved her friends, her Quaker school, and the happy days of plantation work like spinning, weaving, and soapmaking. She hated to leave familiar Virginia, but it was thrilling to think of going to the big city, too. Dolley's main fear was how she, and especially her younger siblings, would get along without Mother Amy, a slave who had been their nurse from the day each one was born. Mother Amy accepted her freedom. However, she asked to stay with the family she had grown to love dearly. She then began to receive wages for caring for them. It was a great comfort to Dolley and her brothers and sisters to know this woman, who had been like a second mother to them, would join them in Philadelphia. Dolley would face many changes in her life, but she met them all with the resolve to cling to the old while welcoming the new adventures.

curing: Preserving by using salt

Philadelphia

Life was very different in Philadelphia. Instead of living on acres of green rolling hills, they had just a small piece of land. Instead of a **stately** home with tall ceilings, their new home had fewer rooms with low ceilings. They didn't have barns full of cured hams and other food they had grown. When Dolley stepped outside, she was in the midst of a **bustling** city with shops everywhere, carriages going by, and women dressed in elegant dresses and hats. It was so unlike the **drab** Quaker style of dress, and it fascinated her. She attended picnics and teas and rode out to the country to visit new friends. She loved entertaining her friends and still went to Quaker meetings regularly.

stately: Fine

bustling: Busy

drab: Dull

Dolley had lived in Philadelphia for four years when the Constitutional Convention met there to create a strong government. She watched as George Washington, Benjamin Franklin, Robert Morris, Alexander Hamilton, Edmond Randolph, the governor of Virginia, and others met

to discuss the new Constitution. She also met a short, good-looking young man from Virginia named James Madison, well-respected for his expert knowledge. The people began to hear of the *Federalist Papers*, a series of articles written by John Jay, Alexander Hamilton, and James Madison, which explained why a Constitution was needed. The people read these articles, and soon the Constitution was **ratified**.

Dolley Marries

Dolley was friendly and cheerful. Everyone who met her loved her. She was quite pretty, and many young men wished to marry her, but she always said no. Finally, John Todd kept persisting, and Dolley said yes. Todd was a good Quaker man, honest, intelligent, and industrious. He owned a successful law practice. John and Dolley were married in January 1790, and in two years their first child was born, a son. Another son was born a year or so later. Dolley loved sewing and cooking. She enjoyed her family life.

ratified: Approved

Mother Amy died about the time Dolley's father died in 1792. Her father had not done well financially because he had no experience running a store. Mother

Amy deeply loved the family and had collected wages all those years but had saved her money. She lovingly left it all to Mrs. Payne to help care for the children when her husband died.

Yellow Fever

All went well until **yellow fever** broke out in Philadelphia. No one at the time understood what caused it or how to prevent its spread.

> **yellow fever:** A virus transmitted by a mosquito

People fled the city, but many people died. John insisted Dolley leave with the children and her mother. However, he returned to the city to care for others and do what law work he could. When his parents became ill with the fever, he nursed them. Sadly, they died, and then John caught the fever. He felt he had to see Dolley. He forced himself, though on the point of death, to go to her. When he arrived at the home where she was staying, she ran to him; he died in her arms just hours later. Dolley became sick, and so did her two-month-old son. After a long time, Dolley recovered, but her baby son did not. When the epidemic was over, Dolley and others returned to the city to their abandoned homes to start life over again.

James Madison

One day, James Madison, who had taken notice of Dolley, came to visit. He was friendly and intelligent. They saw each other often. A rumor began to go around that Dolley and James were engaged. General Washington's wife Martha asked Dolley if she was engaged to Madison:

> "If it is so, do not be ashamed to confess it. Rather be proud. He will make thee a good husband and all the better for being so much older. We both approve of it. The esteem and friendship existing between Mr. Madison and my husband is very great and we would wish thee to be happy."[18]

Dolley wasn't sure. She decided to take a trip by stagecoach to Virginia to have time to think. She ended up writing to Madison to tell him she would marry him. On her wedding day, Dolley wrote to a friend, "I give my hand to the man of all others I most admire."[19] They were married on September 15, 1794.

Political Differences

When James and Dolley married, there were two political parties in America, though not the same as those we have today. The Federalists

believed in a strong federal government. The Democrats thought common people should have more power. James Madison was a Democrat, as was Thomas Jefferson. When Thomas Jefferson was elected President of the United States, he made James Madison his Secretary of State. The Madisons had to leave their beautiful home named Montpelier in the Blue Ridge Mountains of Virginia and move to Washington, D.C. Dolley was a wonderful hostess and did much entertaining. Jefferson's wife had died, and he asked Dolley to be the nation's official hostess.

The United States greatly expanded its territory during this time. James Madison helped buy the Louisiana Territory, and Dolley put on a huge celebration. She and her helpers made cakes and served hundreds of people. The Northwest Territory was added, as well, as a result of the expedition led by William Clark and Meriwether Lewis. Before they set out, Dolley hosted a big dinner in their honor.

First Lady

In 1809, James Madison was elected President of the United States. Dolley Madison was the First Lady. She continued as hostess for many events. She loved wearing pretty dresses like she had dreamed of doing as a Quaker child. She wore a yellow velvet dress at her husband's **inauguration**.

inauguration: Ceremony in which a person takes office

When Jefferson left the White House, he took all his lovely

furniture back to his home in Monticello. Dolley said, “I believe the President’s House belongs to the people and should be beautiful and have things of its own.”[20] Congress approved this idea and gave money for furniture. Dolley and an **architect** began to decorate the house. Dolley used many mirrors to make the rooms appear larger. She picked out chairs, sofas, a piano, a guitar, and a parrot. Yes, a parrot! He was brightly colored, talkative, and adored by children and all her guests. Her favorite touch was a large painting of George Washington done by the famous artist Gilbert Stuart, which she hung in the dining room.

architect: Person who designs buildings

Dolley was very popular. Women of the country began copying things she did, including her style of clothes and her dinners. Ice cream was new back then, but Dolley made it popular. Dolley and James had no children except Dolley’s first son from her first marriage. She did love children, though, and liked making them happy. She started an Easter egg roll on the front lawn of the Capitol building every Easter, which is still done to this day, but now on the lawn of the White House. She also helped start an orphanage. She even made clothes for the children in the orphanage. Madison was elected a second time; people said Dolley helped him win. They described her as “uniting to all the elegance and polish of fashion, the unadulterated simplicity, frankness, warmth, and friendliness of her native character.”[21] Yes, she was loved by all!

Dolley Saves George Washington

Dolley will always be remembered for what she did on August 24, 1814. The British landed by the Potomac River with the intent of burning the city of Washington. James told Dolley he felt he needed to be with the army and asked if she was afraid to stay alone with a guard to protect her. She was not. He asked her to try to pack government papers in trunks to save them and send them to a safe place.

Soon after James left, Dolley heard the boom of cannons in the distance. She called to her guard to help her pack Mr. Madison's papers. She packed up their silver and valuables to take with her if she had to flee. The next morning, a soldier brought her a note from James telling her to leave at once. Just as she was about to escape, she remembered the portrait of General Washington. She told her aide John to take it off the wall. John said the frame was nailed to the wall and would not come off. Dolley told him to break the frame. She gave the portrait to two men with orders to take it to New York to a safe place. George Washington's famous portrait was saved and still exists today, hanging on a wall in the White House!

Here Come the British

Dolley left quickly in a carriage through streets jammed with **frenzied** people trying to escape danger. The British set fire to the Capitol building and burned down the Library of Congress with all its valuable books. They went next to the President's house and piled up Dolley's lovely furniture and Madison's books in the center of the room and set them on fire. Dolley spent the first night in a soldier's camp. The next day she drove to a place where she had arranged to meet James. They talked, but a messenger told him his life was in danger and he must flee. He and his guards went to the woods. Dolley disguised herself as a poor country woman and left in a farm wagon. Two men went with her for protection and drove through the countryside for two days.

frenzied: Excited and uncontrolled

Meanwhile, a fierce hurricane hit Washington, D.C., ripped roofs off houses, and tipped over British cannons. **Torrents** of rain fell for hours, extinguishing the flames of fires the British had set. Finally, the orders came for the British soldiers to leave the city. Washington was a pile of rubble and ashes. Dolley returned to the city and drove to her sister's house, which was still standing. Here she was reunited with James. They were together and safe. Very soon after, a treaty was signed with the British, and the War of 1812 ended.

torrents: Violent rains causing flooding

Washington had to be rebuilt. Nevertheless, Dolley still found time to have parties and help the **orphans**. At the end of James' second term as President, they went home to their beautiful Montpelier which covered between three to four thousand acres, their herds of cattle, and their spacious home. They entertained the famous Layfayette, French friend to America, when he returned for a visit. A visiting Frenchman once said, "Everyone loves Mrs. Madison."[22] Dolley's response may be the secret of her life-long popularity with people: "Mrs. Madison loves everybody," she quickly said.[23]

orphans: Children whose parents had died

5

Florence Nightingale – The Lady with the Lamp

1854–1856	From England to the Crimean War

Nursing had a bad reputation in England in the mid-1800s. Often, women who became nurses could not find work anywhere else. They were not properly trained, either. Hospitals were filthy; only poor people came to them. Rich people were doctored in their homes. That was the atmosphere in which Florence grew up.

Who Was Florence Nightingale?

Florence Nightingale was born on May 12, 1820, in Florence, Italy. Her parents were from England but were traveling when she was born, and they named her after the city where she was born. During the winter months, the family lived in London. In the summer, they lived in Derbyshire in a large stone house called Lea Hurst. Florence spent her growing-up days playing nurse. When she was a bit older, she began nursing sick animals.

One day while Florence was playing in her yard, the old gardener came to her carrying his dog. A fox had just bitten the dog and torn his leg open. The man knew Florence was always playing nurse and hoped she could help his pet. In a few days under Florence's care, the dog was well again! The gardener began to tell all the neighbors what Florence had done. Soon, people were bringing her their sick pets and even farm

animals. Mr. Nightingale allowed Florence to use a corner of the greenhouse to **accommodate** her "animal hospital." Florence had a dream to be a real nurse one day.

The Nightingales did a lot of traveling, so their father taught Florence and her sister at home. Every year, Florence looked forward to her time at Lea Hurst. Her mother often sent her to bring food to the country people in the village. Florence would take time to visit with them all and care for any who were sick. She took baskets of fresh eggs, cream, and fruit to them. She loved to talk with older folks and rock babies while visiting with their mothers. The village people said, "Miss Flo can cure sick people better than medicine."[24] Florence didn't tell her parents about her visits to the sick. She was afraid they would make her stop.

accommodate: Make room for

One night a neighboring farmer begged Mr. Nightingale to have Miss Florence come with him because his son Georgie had hurt his knee. He said the neighbors all knew how Florence was skilled in caring for the sick. Florence hurried past her astonished father to help little Georgie. She stayed by his bedside that night and each day returned to change his bandages. She always knew how to comfort those in pain. Soon Georgie's knee had healed.

Florence told her parents she wanted to work in a hospital helping sick and hurt people. They were quite upset, telling her that "nice" young ladies did not work in hospitals. In those days, that was true. Hospitals were dirty, crowded places. There was no nursing training available. Her father assured her she would not ever need to work. The family was wealthy. Florence did not care about the money. She was not interested in fancy parties. She wanted to help people.

Then Mr. Nightingale's mother became extremely ill. Florence offered to care for her. The family was amazed at their grandmother's quick recovery. "I'd never have lived had it not been for my sweet Florence," her grandmother declared.[25] Florence constantly prayed that the Lord would use this to help her family understand her desire to be a nurse.

Dr. Elizabeth Blackwell

The Nightingales attended many fancy parties. They were even invited to the Royal Palace by Queen Victoria, who was only one year older than Florence. One young man, Richard Milnes, begged Florence to marry him. Florence did love Richard but would not give up her

dream of being a nurse. Florence felt God was calling her to a life of service, not one of parties and ease. Richard finally told her she had to choose between her work and him. With tears, Florence told him, "I was born to do a special work. I must give up everything else — even you, Richard."[26] She wrote in her diary, "I am thirty, the age at which Christ began his mission. Now no more childish things, no more vain things, no more love, no more marriage. Now Lord, let me think only of Your will."[27] Her family was shocked and disappointed in her.

Then Florence had the opportunity to meet Dr. Elizabeth Blackwell who was visiting from America. She was the first American female medical doctor, and Florence was inspired by meeting her. She told Florence about a hospital in Germany that taught nursing. Finally, Florence's parents reluctantly allowed her to go.

Florence Goes to Nursing School

The hospital in Germany was run by a doctor and his wife. Florence loved the work. She wrote to her parents that she had to get up at 5:00 each morning. Florence was eager to learn everything she could. The doctors trained her to give medicines and assist with surgeries. The children especially loved Florence. She was so cheerful and fun to be around! When Florence left the hospital, the head doctor said, "We have never had a nurse as intelligent and skillful as Miss Nightingale."[28]

When Florence returned to London, she was offered a good job running a

hospital for women. Florence made it her mission to improve cleanliness practices at the hospital, which significantly lowered the death rate of patients. One patient wrote her, "You were our sunshine."[29] The doctors asked Florence to train other girls to be nurses. This had been Florence's dream. Before she could start that job, however, war broke out.

Crimean War

Russia was trying to take land from Turkey. England and France sided with Turkey. War broke out in a place called Crimea, right across the Black Sea from Turkey. English soldiers prepared to head off to war. In a few weeks, though, troubling reports came out. A newspaperman had been to the battlefields in Turkey. He reported, "More than a thousand men were killed or wounded in the first battles. A thousand more are sick and dying with fever. The Army doctors are working hard. But there is no one to take care of the sick men."[30] English people were alarmed at this report. They begged the War Department to send help for their men.

Sir Sidney Herbert was head of the War Department. He happened to be an old friend of Florence. He had heard glowing reports of her

nursing skills and wrote asking her for help. "I know that you will come to a wise decision. God grant that it may be in accordance with my hopes," Sir Herbert wrote.[31] Florence pondered her answer and decided, "If she were needed, she would accept. This was truly the service of the Lord."[32] She decided she would take 40 nurses with her and leave in one week. Florence purchased uniforms and supplies for the nurses. Her father, mother, and sister came to London to help her prepare to leave. Florence was famous now, and her family was, at long last, proud of her.

Choosing Nurses

Florence now had to find enough good nurses who were willing to face the hardships awaiting them. Newspapers reported the story about Florence recruiting nurses to go to Crimea. On October 21, 1854, they boarded a ship and left. The next day, London newspapers wrote, "The prayers of all England go with them."[33] The trip lasted more than a month. Many of the nurses were seasick. The ship arrived at Constantinople, across the Black Sea from Crimea. The ship's captain pointed out the hospital to Florence. It had been used as barracks but had been empty for years until the Army began using it for wounded soldiers — empty, that is, except for dirt and rats. Rats? The nurses cringed to think of it. Florence silently prayed, "Now our work begins. Stay near to us, Lord."[34]

No one met them as they carried their heavy luggage up a steep hill. Just as they were beginning to despair, another ship arrived carrying wounded men. Some could hardly walk, and some were too sick to even move. The nurses soon forgot all about their troubles. A sailor told Florence that hundreds of men were killed or wounded, and plenty more were to arrive soon. The nurses began helping the frail men up the hill.

When they got to the hospital, there were no beds or even blankets for the men to lie on. The building was bleak and cold. The food was sparse; there was hardly any water available. Florence went to the Army officer in charge asking what he wanted the nurses to do. He was furious with the War Department for **inferring** that he was not giving good care to the men. He was even more furious that they had sent women, of all things! He told her the Army had never needed women and did not need them now. The nurses would have to wait until he decided he needed their help.

inferring: Implying

Supper for the nurses that night was dry bread and tea. All 40 of them crowded into a small room to sleep on hard wooden benches. Florence offered to sleep in the closet. It was tiny, but this way she could stay up later than the others to work. She began writing letters.

Florence wrote to Sidney Herbert in London: "The doctors are doing their best. But there is no medicine or decent food. There are no beds. These brave men lie without care. We must find a way to help them …"[35]

The next morning, Florence had an idea. The Army officers did not want women nurses, but perhaps they would accept women cooks. Florence and her nurses lit a fire, scrubbed the pots and pans, and began making soup and hot tea. Then they brought broth to the sick men, who were so appreciative when the nurses fed them. The doctors changed their minds when they saw how useful the nurses were and decided to let them stay. Florence had the nurses start sewing sacks together and stuffing them with straw to make beds for the men. She set up boilers and paid some women from the village to wash the wounded men's clothes and bedding.

More and more men were brought in from the battle. Florence worked harder than anyone. She wrote letters for the soldiers to their families in England. She flooded the War Department with letters requesting warm blankets, clothes, medicine, and bandage supplies. She emphasized that men were dying for lack of these things. Every night Florence would walk through the long rows of men, carrying a lamp to light her way. Many soldiers could not sleep because of pain and sickness. They began to watch for her light and called her "The Lady with the Lamp." That is how she got her nickname.

Florence showed compassion to all the soldiers. If one was fearful about an operation, she would promise to stay by his side. One soldier said,

"She was so brave, she gave us all courage."[36] Another wrote, "What comfort we felt to see her. We lay in the hospital by the hundreds…. We kissed her shadow as she passed."[37]

One night Florence ran out of oil for her lamp, but that did not stop her from making her rounds. She found a young boy sobbing. He told her he was homesick and that he was only 13 years old. His name was Bobby Robinson. Florence told him that when he was better, he could stay there and help her run errands and bring men food. He did get better, and there was not anything he would not do for "The Lady with the Lamp." He was proud to have the duty of polishing her lamp and keeping it filled with oil. He never let it go out again.

Supplies Arrive

The War Department finally sent Florence the supplies she had requested. The soldiers got better so much faster after that. Florence had written to Queen Victoria as well and received this response: "Your goodness and devotion has been observed with highest admiration. Please tell the soldiers that their Queen thinks of them and prays for them every day."[38] The war finally ended with a victory for England and

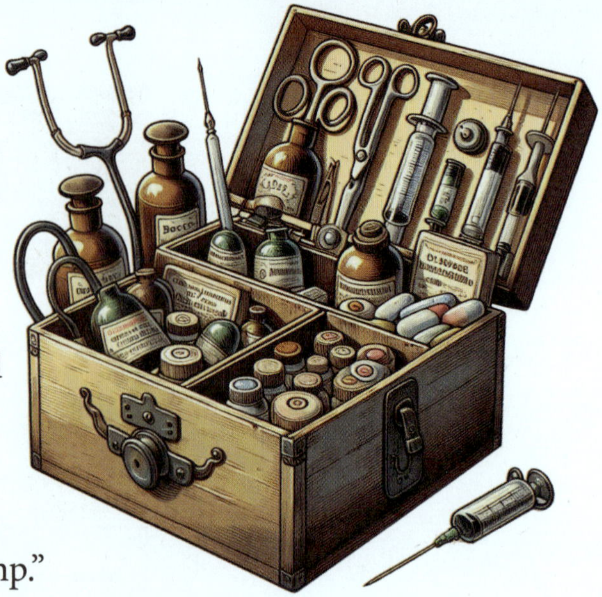

Turkey. Florence took a few days to visit the battlefields in Crimea. Whenever she passed by soldiers, they cheered her.

A few days later, Florence came down with the dreaded fever and fainted. Soldiers carried her to the hospital; Bobby was by her side. Soldiers began praying for their beloved "Lady with the Lamp." People in England began praying for her as well. At last, she recovered, although she was still very weak. The doctors advised her to go home and rest, but she continued to care for her wounded soldiers until they were all able to go home. One of the other nurses wrote, "We all worked long and hard during the war. We were always tired. Only Miss Nightingale never seemed tired. Her voice was always soft. Her smile was beautiful. She kept us all working together."[39]

Home at Last

Florence was home at last at her beloved Lea Hurst. The English people collected money for Florence as a gift of appreciation for all her efforts. She used the money to start a school to train nurses. Florence herself planned the course of studies and chose the first girls to be trained. It was named *The Nightingale School*. She taught them about the human body, nutrition, and different illnesses. They were the very first trained nurses. Soon other nursing schools were started not only in England

but all over the world. Florence's dream was coming true. Although Florence was often sick after the war, it did not stop her from fulfilling her dream and training others. Florence is still known as the world's first great nurse and serves as an inspiration for young people aspiring to give their lives to help the sick and wounded.

6

Kate Shelley – The Girl Who Saved a Train

July 6, 1881	Moingona, Iowa

Railroad transportation came to Iowa in the late 1840s. Iowa had approximately 2,683 miles of tracks by 1870. Railroads helped expand the population by bringing new settlers to Iowa. They were instrumental in providing towns with dairy products, meat, and grain, as well as coal, farm implements, salt, and clothes.

Who Was Kate Shelley?

Kate Shelley was born on September 25, 1864, in County Tipperary, Ireland. Her parents, Michael and Margaret, **immigrated** to the United States when Kate was a baby in 1865. The family didn't have much money. They were looking for a better chance to prosper. They settled into a homestead on Honey Creek in Boone County, Iowa.

immigrated: Moved to a new country

The Homestead Act of 1860, signed into law by President Abraham Lincoln, gave citizens or future citizens up to 160 acres of public land, provided they live on it, improve it, and pay a small registration fee. Often immigrants would take advantage of this provision. Kate's father

built the family a house that overlooked Honey Creek. Here he hoped to become a farmer. Four more children were born into their family — James, Mayme, Margaret, and John. The family worked together to build their little farm. They had hogs, chickens, and a milk cow. They struggled to grow crops, too, but had trouble making ends meet.

Michael took a job to help **supplement** the family's income. He worked for the Chicago and North Western Railroad. He started as a **section hand** and later was promoted to **crew chief**. He was responsible for maintaining the tracks and bridges close to his home. This is where Kate grew up, listening to the chug of the passing trains daily. Kate knew all the schedules of the various types of trains that frequented the tracks near her home. The Des Moines River Bridge was close by. The trains crossed Honey Creek over this bridge.

supplement: Add to

section hand: Laborer who laid and maintained railroad tracks

crew chief: Manager

Trouble Comes

Life was hard for the Shelley family, but they loved each other and enjoyed many good times together. When Kate was only 13, her father died unexpectedly, and life became much more difficult for her

mother. Less than one year later, Kate's ten-year-old brother James drowned while swimming in the Des Moines River. Her mother was, of course, **devastated** and never quite recovered from these losses. Kate, therefore, being the oldest child, took over more responsibility daily for the children and running the farm. She was very capable, and as a result of the family tragedies, grew up more quickly than most girls her age.

The Storm

One day, as 15-year-old Kate brought in the laundry from the clothesline, she could sense a storm was brewing. The air turned cold, the clouds were gathering, and the sky grew dark. Then it began to thunder. Lightning flashed across the sky. Rain poured down in torrents. Kate and her **siblings** watched as Honey Creek began to rise and started to overflow its banks. "The animals!" cried Kate. She ran outside to let the animals out of the barn. If the water rose much higher and they were trapped in the barn, they could drown. She ran through the mud and shooed

devastated: Overcome with grief

siblings: Brothers and sisters

the animals up the hill to higher ground. She tucked the baby pigs under her arms and brought them inside the house. She was drenched when she got back inside. After changing into dry clothes, she ran to the window to keep an eye on the rising water. It was in the yard now, coming closer to the house. When lightning lit up the sky, she tried to see how the bridge over Honey Creek was holding up.

Over supper, Kate and her siblings discussed the possible dangers. They were worried about the men who worked on the railroad. At midnight, an express passenger train always crossed over that bridge. The Chicago and North Western railroad, which used the bridge, always sent out a pusher engine called "Old No. 12" from Moingona to check the tracks. A pusher engine was a railway locomotive that temporarily assists a train that requires additional power or traction to climb a steep bank. There was one long bridge over the Des Moines River and a shorter bridge over Honey Creek that went right past Kate's house.

The Pusher Engine

The storm continued to rage as the rains poured down. Shortly after 11 p.m., Kate and her family heard the pusher engine coming down the tracks to check the bridges ahead of the Midnight Express train. Suddenly the crew began to ring the

engine's bell wildly, and then everyone heard a terrifying crack. Kate knew at once this meant the bridge had **collapsed**, sending the four men riding the pusher into the now-roaring Honey Creek. The flash flood caused by the heavy rains had washed out the support **trestles**. Then, a horrifying thought struck Kate. The passenger train was due in less than an hour! She ran for her jacket and her father's railroad lantern that he had used so many times. Kate's mom protested, "It's too dangerous, Kate!" Her mother pleaded with her but to no avail. Kate said she had to go. Men were fighting the waters now, and soon, the passenger train would be at the bridge. Kate reminded her mother that if it were her father down there, she would want someone to go try to help. She couldn't bear to do nothing. Her mother reluctantly agreed and promised she would be praying for Kate's safety.

collapsed: Fallen down

trestles: Sloping supports used to hold up bridges

The Dangerous Journey

Her yard was already too flooded for Kate to cross it. She would have to take an alternative path behind her house. She would meet up with

the tracks where they ran through the hilly region. Water cascaded down the hills like a mini-waterfall as Kate scrambled over fallen tree limbs. At times, she sank in the heavy mud, but she held fast to her father's lantern and made her way to the tracks. Running along the tracks, she made it to the broken bridge over Honey Creek. Kate heard someone call out amid the roaring of the flowing waters. When the lightning flashed, she saw a man holding to the branches of a treetop sticking out above the waters. The storm was howling. It was hard to hear, but she thought she made out two men's voices. Kate hollered as loud as she could for them to hang on. "I'm getting help!" she bellowed, and swung her lantern back and forth to let them know someone knew of their **plight**.

Kate began to run toward the Moingona station. She just had to get there before the Midnight Express. A strong wind blew out her lantern's small flame, but Kate knew she had to keep going. The flashes of lightning helped her to see. She had to cross the river to reach the station. She got to the high bridge over the nearby Des Moines River, almost 200 feet above the flood waters. Pedestrian traffic was discouraged by the railroad in good weather, and walkways on the Des Moines River Bridge had been **dismantled**. She looked at the long wooden bridge before her and

plight: Dangerous situation

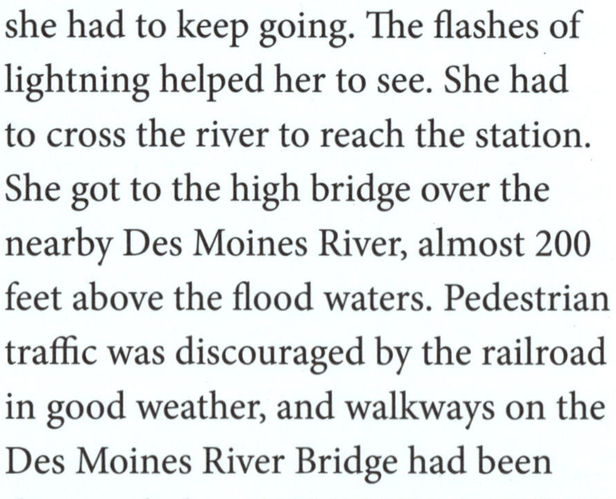

dismantled: Torn down

saw boards were missing. Kate would have been afraid to cross this bridge even in daylight. She was terribly frightened but knew lives were at stake, and no one else knew the bridge had collapsed. She thought of the men in the icy creek fighting for their lives and the passengers coming on that train, unaware they were headed for sure death.

Kate dropped to her knees and began **gingerly** crawling, looking for gaps in the boards to avoid falling through. It was nearly a 700-foot span across the bridge. She soon had painful splinters in her hands and knees from the rough boards. The nails sticking up tore her skirt. The winds were so strong she had to grip tightly to the steel rails to keep from being blown over the side. Fallen trees and logs floating in the rising river **jostled** against the bridge, making it shake. When she was about halfway over the bridge, a huge bolt of lightning showed a massive log heading down the river straight towards her. Kate began to pray. Just then, the swirling river pulled the log under. Kate felt it scrape the walkway as it disappeared into the dark, churning water.

gingerly: Cautiously

jostled: Bumped

It was almost midnight. Kate, though almost faint from fright, knew she must go on. Time was running out. Finally, her hand touched land. She had crossed the bridge. The station was less than half a mile down the road. Kate broke into a run. Her head was aching and her throat burned from running, but she saw the station lights just ahead.

At the Station

Kate, tattered and muddy, wildly pushed open the door, dripping water everywhere. She tried to speak but couldn't at first. She finally managed to croak out the words, "The engine went down in Honey Creek. Stop the express!"[40] Then she collapsed into a heap on the floor. One of the men thought she must be crazy, but the station master knew Kate and her family. He rushed to the **telegraph** and sent an urgent message to Ogden, the station just before Moingona: "STOP EXPRESS … BRIDGE OUT … STOP EXPRESS."[41] Another man grabbed a lantern and ran outside to alert the train by flagging it down, just in case the message didn't get to them on time.

Two hundred passengers were on the train that night. Ogden got the

telegraph: Machine for transmitting messages from a distance by a wire

message just in time. It actually was the last telegraph message transmitted that night because shortly after it was sent, the storm knocked out the telegraph lines. Kate then told the men about the man from the pusher engine she had seen holding onto a tree, trying to keep from drowning. She told them she thought she had heard two men's voices calling for help. The men asked the exhausted Kate if she could lead them to where the bridge was down. This time, however, Kate rode the engine with the rescue team, crossing the same bridge she had just crawled over. The engine, of course, stopped before reaching the broken bridge over Honey Creek.

They spotted the men but could not reach them from that side of the creek. They hollered for the men to hold on a bit longer. Kate led the rescue party to the hills behind her house and through the woods to a bridge farther upstream. There they crossed the creek and rescued the exhausted men! Only two of the four had survived — Edgar Wood and Adam Agar. Kate saved more than 200 lives that night.

Home at Last

When she finally got home, Kate changed into dry clothes and fell exhausted into bed. When she awoke after a long sleep, neighbors, friends, and newspaper

reporters crowded around her to hear about her **perilous** journey. Soon newspapers all over the country were telling her story. The Chicago and North Western Railroad gave Kate $100, along with a half-barrel of flour, a load of coal, and a lifetime pass to use the railroad. **The Order of Conductors** gave Kate a gold watch and chain. Kate instantly became a heroine. She received a gold medal from the state legislature. People raised funds to allow her to attend college and even pay off her struggling family's **mortgage**. Poems and songs were written in her honor.

perilous: Dangerous

The Order of Conductors: Organization representing train conductors in the United States

mortgage: Loan on their home

In 1903, the Chicago and North Western Railroad offered her the position of **station agent** in Moingona, where she worked until she died in 1912. After her death, the train bridge over the Des Moines River was renamed the *Kate Shelley High Bridge*; later a passenger train was named after her — *The Kate Shelley 400.*

station agent: Official and respected representative of the company

7

Annie Oakley – "Little Sureshot"

August 13, 1860– November 3, 1926	Western Ohio

Phoebe Ann Moses was born in a little cabin on August 13, 1860, near Woodland, Ohio. As a young girl, Annie, as she was called, would go hunting with her father Jacob Moses in the woods surrounding their cabin. Her father died of pneumonia when Annie was only five years old. Her mother Susan was left with six young children to care for. She was a nurse, but $1.25 a week wasn't enough to provide for her family. Annie and her brother and sisters did all they could to help by caring for the animals, doing the laundry, working in the vegetable garden, cooking, sewing, and caring for the babies.

Whenever she had free time, Annie loved to wander in the woods. She began making traps from cornstalks and string, something her father had taught her. She would catch birds in the traps and put many meals on the table that way. Annie had often watched her father shoot his gun. She was sure she could shoot as well. One day, she took his rifle down, shot a squirrel, and provided supper. By the time she was 10, she was handling the gun skillfully.

The Orphan House

When Annie was eight, her mother sent her to live with Mr. and Mrs. Crawford Eddington, who ran a home for orphans. Annie helped them in exchange for her room and board. Mrs. Eddington taught her to sew, knit, and embroider, and she would often mend the children's clothes. She helped do chores and cook, but the Eddingtons did not have enough money to pay her. One day, a farmer stopped by to ask if the orphanage had a girl who could do household chores and babysit. He promised to pay her 50 cents a week, saying she would also have the opportunity to attend school. Annie asked the farmer to give her pay to her mother to help care for her siblings, and she rode off with him.

However, it turned out that the farmer and his wife were very mean. They made Annie get up at 4 a.m. to milk the cows and feed the animals. The woman made her work hard all day long. She didn't have any spare time, and they did not let her go to school. One night Annie overheard the farmer and his wife talking about how they never had sent her mother any money at all over the last two years; they just kept telling her mother she was in school and doing fine. That night, Annie decided she would run away after the family was asleep and go home. She ran to a nearby railroad station and caught a train that stopped close to her mother's home.

Home Again

Annie's mother had remarried. Her new husband had purchased a farm. He had borrowed money to do it and was having a hard time earning enough money to pay back the debt. Annie was determined to help. She started hunting again and brought home rabbits, squirrels, and birds for the family to eat. She entered shooting contests and brought in some money that way as well. She bought her shotgun shells from the general store in Greenville.

One day, she brought the owner a gift of six fat quail. She explained that she always tried to hit them in the head so no lead shots could get into the meat. Most **game animals** were killed with shotguns that left tiny pellets in the meat, which had to be picked out before eating. Biting down on a piece of shot could possibly break a tooth. Annie used a rifle and was such a good shot that she killed her birds with one bullet which was easily removed before the bird was cooked. That gave the shop owner an idea. He told her he had a friend who ran a hotel in Cincinnati, 80 miles away. He thought his friend would probably pay her good money for quail shot her way. He was right. The hotel owner provided food for his guests and was happy to find such a supplier. He paid Annie well. She gave most of her money to her stepfather to help pay his debt. One day, he proudly announced he had made the last payment. They now owned the farm. Annie was just 15 years old.

game animals:
Animals hunted in the wild, usually for meat

Meeting Frank

Annie's sister Lydia was married and lived in Cincinnati. She asked Annie to come for a visit. Lydia and her husband Joe took Annie to a shooting gallery. Joe was impressed with how well she shot. They heard about a shooting match that was to take place on Thanksgiving Day, and Annie agreed to enter it. There was a large cash prize for the winner. Her opponent was a man named Frank Butler, who had a reputation for trick shooting. Annie thought he was the most handsome man she had ever seen.

The targets used in the match were clay "pigeons." They were not real pigeons, but round pieces of clay that were thrown into the air. Frank Butler shot first. Then Annie. Both kept hitting their targets without fail until the very last shot; Frank missed. Annie had won! She won the match, and she also won the heart of Frank Butler. He said, "Well done, Miss Moses. I am proud to be beaten by such a good shot."[42] Within a year, Frank and Annie were married.

Performing on Stage

Frank had to be at the theater each evening. He had a partner, Billy, as his assistant for his trick shooting act. They had a white poodle named George. At the end of every performance, Frank would place an apple on George's head and shoot the apple off. One night Billy was sick, so Annie stood in for him. She did all the trick shooting Billy had done, and even shot the apple off George's head! The crowd went wild with cheering. From then on, Annie traveled with Frank. He said she needed a new "**stage name.**" They settled on "Oakley." She would now be known as Annie Oakley. Frank and Annie became the shooting team of Butler and Oakley.

> **stage name:** Made-up name used for performances

Frank soon realized Annie was a better shot than he was, and he decided to be her manager. He would take care of business matters and throw targets — clay pigeons and glass balls — into the air for her to shoot. People began to call Annie "Queen of the Rifle."

Annie Gets Her Name

One night, Annie and Frank were performing at a theater in St. Paul, Minnesota. Annie shot corks out of bottles, snuffed the flames out of burning candles, and shot the end off a cigarette in Frank's mouth. Sitting Bull, the famous Sioux Indian chief who had defeated General Custer at the Battle of Little Bighorn, was watching the show. He insisted on meeting with Annie the following day, and presented her with many gifts, including the moccasins he had worn when fighting Custer. His daughter had died shortly after Little Bighorn. He asked Annie if he could adopt her as his daughter. He was extremely impressed with her shooting skills. She told him she had a stepfather, but why not have another one too? He named her "Watanya Cicilla," which meant "Little Sureshot." That's how Annie got her nickname. Years later, when Sitting Bull died, he left all his possessions to his "Little Sureshot."

Buffalo Bill Cody

In 1885, Annie and Frank met Bill Cody, a former Pony Express rider, army **scout**, and **stagecoach** driver. The Kansas Pacific Railroad hired him to supply meat for its workers who were building the railroad. He killed many buffalo in eight months and earned his name, "Buffalo Bill."

People were so curious about the "Wild West," an expression used for life in the western United States in the late 1800s when it was not well-populated, that Bill had started a show advertised as "A Visit to the Wild West in Three Hours." He took it all over America. It involved hundreds of wild buffalo, deer, elk, horses, and bears, as well as Native Americans, American cowboys, and Mexican cowboys. It was an exciting show of roping, shooting, **lariat** tricks, music, and horsemanship. It also had reenactments of historic events that had happened on the frontier. People could see Pony Express riders, outlaws ambushing coaches, Native American attacks, and of course, Buffalo Bill and his **posse** coming to the rescue with guns blazing. Buffalo Bill said he knew folks would love to see Annie shoot, and Frank was again her manager.

scout: Person who gathers information for the army

stagecoach: Horse-drawn vehicle to transport passengers

lariat: Rope used as lasso

posse: Group of men whom a sheriff asks to help enforce the law

The Show

Annie wore a **buckskin** skirt and shirt and rode a white horse. She would shoot glass balls Frank threw in the air, and then a coin he held between his thumb and forefinger. When Frank held up a playing card, Annie would shoot through the hearts or clubs on it. Buffalo Bill's Wild West show was quite popular. His **troupe** appeared in many cities.

buckskin: Skin of male deer

troupe: Group of performers who travel together

Mark Twain: Famous American author

Wales: Small country on the west coast of England

After a show in New York one night, Buffalo Bill said **Mark Twain** asked him to take the Wild West Show to England so people there could see what the West was like. They set out by ship one day in 1887. The Prince and Princess of **Wales** came to see the show in London. Later, Queen Victoria of England, came bringing with her kings and queens from other countries. To show her appreciation for the performance, the Queen stood up and bowed her head to the American flag. Annie was very popular in England. Four men, not knowing she was married as she went by the last name of Oakley, asked her to marry them. One man sent her his picture and asked to marry her. She jokingly shot some holes through the photograph and returned it to him, saying she was happily married.

After England, they performed in Germany. The **Kaiser's** son walked up and asked Annie if he could be the helper to hold something in his mouth. A little nervously, Annie agreed and skillfully shot the end off of it. The crowd cheered wildly.

Frank and Annie did many shows in America and Europe. Once in Vienna, Austria, a rich **Baroness** asked Annie to do a show to raise money to benefit orphans. Remembering the orphans from her days helping the Eddingtons, Annie gladly did the show, and much money was raised. The Baroness gave Annie a large bag of gold coins, but Annie gave it all to the orphans. Pleased, the Baroness then sent Annie a big diamond pin.

Kaiser: The German ruler

Baroness: Wife of an Austrian ruler

Back in America, during one summer alone, the Wild West Show was seen by over six million people and profited a million dollars. By that time, Annie was one of the most famous women in America. Annie and Frank purchased a home in Nutley, New Jersey, around Christmastime, 1893. Annie decided she wanted guests, so she sent an invitation to *Forest and Stream* magazine. It read, "I beg of all friends and sportsmen not to pass by without stopping. No

matter if they shoot a $30 or a $300 gun, their welcome will be just the same."[43] Soon, however, Frank and Annie were back on the road with the Nutley Amateur Circus. They produced the show to benefit the Red Cross, one of their favorite **charities**.

A Terrible Crash

One night in 1901, Annie and Frank were traveling on the Wild West train from Charlotte, North Carolina, to Danville, Virginia. They were awakened by a horrific crash and thrown out of their beds. The show train had smashed into a freight train! Both trains were almost destroyed, and nearly all the Wild West horses were killed. No people died, but many were hurt. Annie injured her hands and back and had to wear a brace on her right leg for a long time.

charities: Organizations to help those in need

Frank and Annie went to their home in Nutley for Annie to recover. Once she was better, she began teaching others how to shoot, and she appeared at many charity shows. She gave thousands of dollars to veterans' hospitals. When World War I began, she and Frank visited army camps, putting on shows and giving shooting lessons. She told the young soldiers, "If I can shoot, you boys can shoot."[44] When the war ended, she performed at a charity circus to raise money for wounded soldiers. Annie died quietly in 1926, at the home of a friend in Ohio. Frank, her beloved husband, died 18 days later. They are buried side-by-side in Brock cemetery in Ohio, just a few miles from where "Little Sureshot" was born.

8

Clara Barton – The Angel of the Battlefield

1821–1912	From North Oxford, Massachusetts to Battlefields Everywhere

In the early 1800s in America, nobody understood that germs caused disease. Doctors didn't know they needed to wash their hands between working on different patients. Medical instruments weren't sterilized. Doctors often treated many diseases by "bleeding" the patient. This meant they drew blood from the patient, attempting to drain out "bad blood." They hoped the patient would improve, but many got weak instead and died from the treatments. By the time of the Civil War, things began to improve slightly, but infectious diseases still spread quickly, and many soldiers died of disease rather than wounds.

Who Was Clara Barton?

Clara Barton was born on Christmas Day, 1821, in Oxford, Massachusetts, at her family's large farm. Clara was the youngest of five children. She was quite a bit younger than her siblings, and it almost seemed they were all like parents to Clara. Her sisters and brothers loved teaching her. Her oldest sister Dorothy taught her to read before she turned three. Stephen taught her arithmetic. David taught her how to ride a horse and shared his love of animals and carpentry with her. Sally helped teach her reading and writing. Her mother taught her sewing and cooking. Her favorite

teacher of all, though, was her father. He taught her, surprisingly enough, military tactics. He had been a captain who fought under Mad Anthony Wayne in the American War of Independence. He told her stories about lying in a frozen swamp drinking water from his horse's hoof print, and other adventures. She learned about infantry, cavalry, and artillery. She and her father mapped out military battles on the floor, using grains of corn for soldiers, and together, they fought the war again. The knowledge Clara's father taught her from an early age enabled her to face and navigate a battlefield. Her horsemanship helped her to escape capture.

David's Injury

When Clara was 11 years old, her beloved brother David fell off a barn roof and was seriously hurt. Clara pleaded to be allowed to help him. It amazed her family that she seemed to have an instinct for how to care for him and make him comfortable. Bit by bit she began to take over all of his care. David was ill for two years, and she stayed with him day and night during that time, leaving only for short breaks to ride her horse, Billy. When David recovered, Clara didn't have anyone else

to care for, until one of her father's hired hands came down with smallpox. Smallpox was highly contagious and spread through the village. Clara nursed each patient. She came down with it herself, but recovered quickly and immediately began nursing others. Caring for sick people made Clara shine. It was a driving passion for her to serve ill or wounded people.

Schoolteacher

When Clara was 17, she applied to be a schoolteacher in a little one-room schoolhouse in North Oxford. She had 40 students of all ages. Four of the boys were almost as old as she was. Very nervously, she stood before the class and read to them from the Bible, Matthew chapter 5: "Blessed are the merciful, for they shall obtain mercy." She glanced at the boys as she read it. At lunchtime, she joined the boys by pitching a ball, thankful for the skill David had taught her. The boys were amazed that their teacher could pitch better than they could and run faster, too.

They played other games as well. Clara excelled in them all and thus won the boys' respect. Those four boys soon stayed after school, offering to do errands and chores for her. One of them even carried her books home for her every day. The boys never lost respect for her,

and years later she attended to some of the wounds they received on the battlefield. Clara had respect for them in return:

> "They were faithful to me in school and faithful later to their country, for their blood crimsoned some of the hardest battlefields. I have never seen finer boys."[45]

Clara Starts a School and Goes to College

Over the next ten years, Clara taught at many schools. She never had trouble with unruly children because of the way she treated them. When her brothers started a mill, Clara opened a school for the mill workers' children and taught them for several years while still living at home. Clara enrolled in Hamilton College in New York, thinking she needed to learn more to be a better teacher.

After graduating, she was visiting a college friend who lived in Bordentown, New Jersey. Noticing rough-looking boys hanging around during the day, she discovered there was no opportunity for them to attend school. Schools were not free in New Jersey. She arranged a meeting with the Bordentown school board and offered to start a public school and teach without pay. She opened the school in July with six boys. The following day 20 boys came, and in two weeks there were 55.

Then girls began coming too. Soon the school was crowded. The town officials were pleased and began paying her a salary. The enrollment quickly increased to 200 students, with 400 more wanting to come. The town voted to build a bigger school, but then chose a man to run it, not Clara, saying the job was too hard for a woman. Clara figured if she had built it and caused it to grow, she should easily handle being the principal. She stayed for a while, but soon decided it was time to move on.

Clara moved to Washington, D.C., and took a high-paying job for the U.S. Patent Office. She often would go to the Library of Congress just to read. She read up on all the political issues facing the country. By 1860, the United States was on the brink of civil war.

Civil War Comes

On April 19, 1861, the Sixth Massachusetts Regiment was bound for Washington, D.C. They were the first unit to answer President Lincoln's call for 75,000 troops. Traveling along Pratt Street in

Baltimore, they were attacked by an angry mob of secessionist Southern sympathizers. The Southerners began throwing bricks and paving stones at the Massachusetts men, and the militia defended itself with their guns. This was the first fighting of the Civil War and came to be known as the Baltimore Riots. Many of these Massachusetts boys were the very ones Clara had taught in her first teaching position! She had helped to equip them with blankets, clothing, and food, using her own money. After the battle, Clara cared for the soldiers wounded in the encounter and it affected her deeply to have personally known some of the boys.

At the Battle of Bull Run, 3,000 Union soldiers were killed or wounded. Clara desperately wanted to be a nurse for these men, but it wasn't considered respectable for a woman to be on the battlefield. She wrote to the War Department, which was the government agency responsible for recruiting, training, and supplying the armed forces, as well as writing **politicians**. Finally, she went to see her 88-year-old father, who had taught her so much about war. He encouraged her and told her nursing would not bring her shame, but respect. His words gave

politicians: People who hold elected office

her the courage she needed, and she doubled her efforts. She even began writing to Union generals. She finally got permission to help treat the wounded in July 1862. She devised a system to transport bandages, clothing, and food from women's groups in New Jersey and Massachusetts to Washington, D.C.

On the Battlefield

The defeat of the Union forces at Cedar Mountain, Virginia, was the first time she went to the battlefront to care for wounded men. Although she had heard about war from her father, it was so much more terrible than she had imagined. She tended to men fearlessly though, not giving thought to the bullets whizzing around her. There weren't enough doctors. Sometimes she used her pocketknife to remove bullets from the men. She bandaged them, gave medicine, assisted with surgeries, and went without sleep for many hours. At the Battle of Chantilly, Clara saw a soldier lying on the ground with his arm badly **mangled**. His shirt was torn mostly off, and he was shivering. Clara went over to tend to him when he flung his good arm around her neck and burst into tears. "Don't you know me? I used to carry your books home from school."[46] He was one of the four tough boys from her very first school!

mangled: Wounded severely

Clara brought comfort to many dying men. Conditions were hard. Sometimes she had to work in driving rain. One night, the rain had flooded her little tent, but she was so exhausted she lay down in the stream running through the tent, propping her head to try to keep it above the water. After two hours of sleep, she arose, feeling rested, wrung out her dripping wet clothes, and went back to attending the wounded.

Antietam was one of the worst battles of the war. A bullet actually ripped the sleeve of her dress, striking and killing the soldier she was nursing. One night Clara found one of the surgeons, Dr. Dunn, in despair. So many men needed immediate attention, and it had gotten dark. He was performing surgery with only a lone candle to provide light. He was distraught that when that candle burned out, he would have to wait till morning, and it would be too late for some of the men. Clara led him to the doorway of the barn where she had just lit some lanterns. Stunned, he asked where they had come from. Clara told him she had brought them with her in her supply wagon and had four full boxes left. He dashed back to work, greatly encouraged.

Years later, when Clara was speaking to a group in the Midwest relating this story, a man ran up to her after her talk and told her, "Madam, I am that doctor. If I did not thank you then, I thank you now."[47] Another surgeon, observing her courage wrote, "In my feeble estimation, General McClellan, with all his laurels, sinks into insignificance beside the true heroine of the age, the angel of the battlefield."[48] That's how she got her nickname that stuck with her for the rest of her life.

After the War

After the war ended, many families wanted to know what had become of their loved ones. People began to hear of Clara Barton and her dedication to the wounded. She now received that respect as her father had **predicted**. She began getting thousands of letters asking if she would help find information about missing soldiers. The government gave her permission to open an office to help identify Union soldiers as missing or dead.

predicted: Told her earlier

A former Union soldier named Dorence Atwater, who had been a prisoner at the Andersonville prison, had been assigned to keep a record of the dead. Conditions in that prison were so terrible that hundreds of men died each day for lack of food or from disease.

The South had scarce provisions for their own soldiers and less for prisoners. Atwater had feared that officials might not want to report all the many deaths, so he had made his own copy of the death records that he smuggled out when he was released from prison. He heard what Clara was trying to do and helped her arrange the list of nearly 13,000 names. When the national cemetery was opened in Andersonville on August 17, 1865, Clara was chosen to raise the flag. She worked for four years tracing missing men, without receiving pay. She began to speak to groups all over the country telling of her wartime experiences to raise her own support.

One night, when she was scheduled to speak, her voice gave out. She was ill and needed a break. Her doctor suggested she go to Europe to get rest since people didn't know her there. Her health finally did improve. War broke out between France and Germany while she was there. She helped out with **relief** work, and it was here she learned of an organization known as the International Red Cross.

relief: Aid for disasters

The Red Cross

Clara met a Swiss businessman, Henri Dunant, who had started an organization to care for all those wounded in times of war, with the help of Dr. Louis Appia, a Swiss surgeon. They chose an emblem to represent the organization. Since it had started in Switzerland, they reversed the Swiss flag, making a red cross on a white field. Hospitals flying the Red Cross flag were to be protected and not fired upon. All nations were invited to a meeting in Geneva, Switzerland, to sign a treaty to agree to the terms.

Clara was greatly impressed by the work of this organization. The Red Cross always distributed all contributions promptly. Wherever a battle occurred, supplies, workers, surgeons, and nurses stood ready to help. She remembered how so many in America's Civil War had been neglected for hours — and poor Dr. Dunn with his one dwindling candle. But America had not joined the Red Cross. When Clara returned to America, she kept in touch with Dr. Appia. She spoke with senators, members of the State Department, and even President Rutherford Hayes, but no one was willing to join the International Red Cross. Finally, President James A. Garfield gave his approval to start the first American chapter.

Two major flood disasters helped to give publicity to the American Red Cross. One occurred in 1882 when the Mississippi River flooded, and the other when the Ohio River flooded in 1884. The American Red Cross, led by Clara Barton, brought food, clothing, and blankets, and even raised $10,000 for crop replacement. Flood victims called Clara an angel. She came to the forefront again during the Johnstown flood, one of the worst catastrophes of the century. A dam broke, releasing 20,000,000 tons of water that devastated the town of Johnstown, Pennsylvania. After the Red Cross constructed houses there for homeless people, some lumber was left over. Clara sent this lumber to Glen Echo, Maryland, near Washington, D.C., and used it to build a headquarters for the Red Cross. It also became her home. The list of disasters she helped with is extensive. When there was a human need, Clara and the Red Cross were there to the rescue.

Clara died on Good Friday, April 12, 1912. The wagon driver transporting her body to Oxford, Massachusetts, was overcome when he found out whose body was in the wagon. Tears welled up in his eyes as he explained, "Why, my father was a **Confederate** soldier at the Battle of Antietam! He was wounded in the neck and was bleeding to death when Miss Barton found

Confederate: Southern

him on the battlefield and bound up his wounds in time to save his life."[49] Clara always helped any soldier, Union or Confederate, black or white, Spanish or American, Christian or Muslim. It is that vision she worked so tirelessly to **impart** to people around the globe.

impart: Pass on to

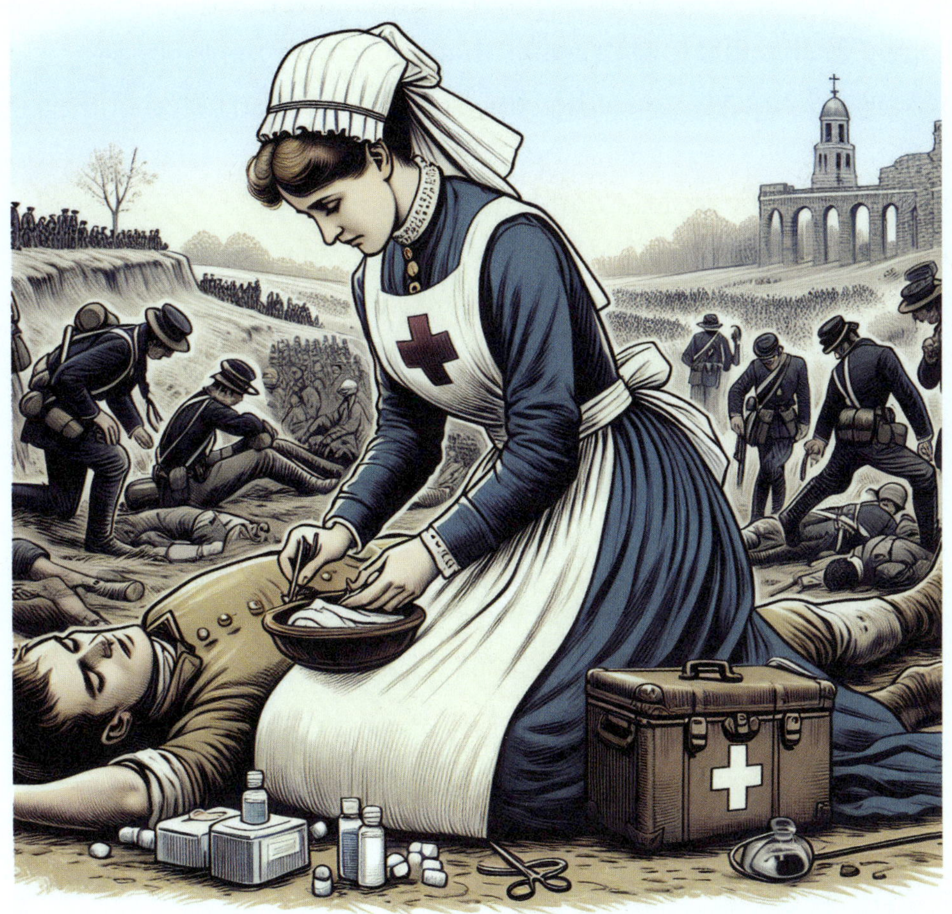

Amelia Earhart – Lady Aviator

1897–1937	Atchinson, Kansas

Amelia Earhart was born in Atchison, Kansas, on July 24, 1897. When Amelia was seven years old, her father took her to the World's Fair in St. Louis, Missouri. Amelia and her younger sister saw a huge roller coaster. When they returned home, they assembled materials to build one themselves. They used wood from an old fence and made wooden tracks that ran from the shed roof to the yard. They greased the wheels of a baby buggy made from an old skate. Amelia volunteered to be the first one to try it out. Down she went, crashing headfirst. This didn't discourage her, though. She adjusted the slope of the tracks and tried again. This time it worked! Amelia loved the feeling of flying through the air. Maybe this experience helped to influence her in later life.

An Airplane

Amelia went to a state fair in Iowa when she was about to enter the eighth grade. She and her sister got their first ride on a Ferris wheel. Amelia loved the thrill of it, but her sister was scared stiff. She saw her first airplane at this fair. Amelia wasn't especially impressed at the time. It was a pretty simple machine. It was only six years after Wilbur and Orville Wright had made their first flight at Kitty Hawk, North Carolina.

After finishing high school, Amelia studied in Philadelphia. Her sister Muriel was attending school in Toronto, Canada. While visiting her, Amelia saw many soldiers. The First World War had started in Europe. Canada had been in the war for quite a while and many Canadian soldiers were wounded. Seeing four soldiers walking about on crutches, Amelia wanted to find a way to help them recover. She became a nurse's aide at the hospital and brought medicine and food to the men. They all loved Amelia and her caring ways. On one of her days off, she and a friend went to the nearby airfield. Amelia was captivated watching a pilot do stunts. She decided that one day, she would fly.

An Air Show

It was Christmas Day, 1920. Amelia had moved back home with her parents, who now lived in California. Amelia and her father were at an air show in Long Beach, California. The pilots were racing and doing all sorts of stunts. Amelia was fascinated and wanted to know how much flying lessons would cost. Her father suggested she take a plane ride before she made any decisions. After all, she might hate it. Three days later, Amelia and her father went to Rogers Field, and Amelia took her first plane ride. The plane had no glass for windows or even a roof. Amelia put on a flying helmet and goggles. A man on the ground spun the propeller — that's how planes were started in those days. Off went the plane as the wind beat across

Amelia's face. She said later, "As soon as we left the ground, I knew I, myself, had to fly."[50]

Flying Lessons

Kinner Airfield was nearby, and there Amelia met Neta Snook, a woman pilot who agreed to give her lessons. It would cost her $1.00 per minute. That was a lot of money in 1921. Amelia determined to do whatever it took to pay for her lessons. The next day, she walked three miles from the **streetcar** to the airfield. She only learned to **taxi** the first day, but it wasn't long before she was flying. Her teacher said she seemed to take to flying naturally. Neta was 24, only a year older than Amelia. They became close friends, and Neta patiently answered Amelia's many questions. Amelia learned how to take off, how to **bank** when she made a turn, and how to pull out of a dive if the engine **stalled**. When the weather was good, Amelia would fly. When the weather was bad, she would study about flying. She also learned how to repair airplanes, which was valuable information for a pilot.

streetcar: Public transportation vehicle on rails

taxi: Move a plane on the runway

bank: Use moveable parts of the wing to turn

stalled: Stopped running

A Plane of Her Own

Amelia's mother was proud of her flying skills and helped her buy a small plane. She painted it yellow and named it the *Canary*. On December 15, 1921, less than one year since her first flying lesson, Amelia took her test, passed, and was officially a pilot. "Nothing on land or sea can be more lovely than the realm of clouds," she said.[51]

When Neta got married, Amelia found a new instructor, an expert named Monte Montijo. He had learned to fly in the army and had also done **stunt work** in movies. Monte taught Amelia to do huge upside-down loops in the air and several other tricks. Amelia flew in some air shows to make money to pay for lessons. Since most pilots were men, she attracted a lot of attention.

stunt work: difficult feats requiring great daring

A Record

Amelia decided she wanted to see how high she could fly. She had an **altimeter** installed in her plane. Since planes had open cockpits, the pilot had to be careful not to run out of oxygen by flying too high. She finally made it to 14,000 feet or three miles. She had set a record for being the first woman to fly that high. Finally, Amelia realized she would have to take a job to support her love of flying.

altimeter: instrument to determine altitude

In 1924, she sold the *Canary* and bought a car, a fancy yellow convertible which she named *Yellow Peril*. She drove her mother across the country to Boston. There she found a job at the Denison House caring for poor children. She loved the job. It was fulfilling to do something that made a difference in the lives of children. However, now she could only fly on weekends.

Across the Sea

Amelia heard of Charles Lindbergh, the first man to fly **solo** across the Atlantic Ocean. It took him a little over 33 hours to fly from Long Island, New York, to Paris, France. A man named George Putnam, a book publisher from New York, was looking for a woman who would be willing to be a passenger in a plane being flown across the Atlantic. He also wanted the woman to be a pilot. Amelia met with George in New York. The offer wasn't as good as she'd hoped. She would not be paid, and a man named Wilmer Stultz would actually do the flying. Stultz would be using instruments to help him fly. Amelia hadn't learned how to use instruments yet as they were very new. Although she'd be called the "captain," Amelia

solo: Alone

would really only be a passenger. This is why she told a friend she decided to go: "When a great adventure's offered you, you don't refuse it, that's all."[52]

The flight was dangerous. Fourteen other people had tried and failed. Two other women were planning on trying it. Amelia had to move quickly if she wanted to be the first woman to do it. The plane, named the *Friendship*, took off from Boston on June 3, 1928. When faced with fog, rain, and wind, they had to land in Canada and wait until the weather was suitable for flying.

They took off again on June 17. After twenty hours, they were getting low on fuel, the fog was thick, and the radio quit working. Without the radio, it was extremely difficult to know where they were. Forty minutes later, however, they spied land and soon were safely on the ground at Burry Port, Wales. So Amelia Earhart was the first woman to fly across the Atlantic. She instantly became famous even though she had not done the flying. People gave her credit for her bravery. She was entertained in London by royalty. On returning to America, crowds gathered to see her and hear her speak. Parades were organized in her honor. President Calvin Coolidge sent her a message of congratulations. Amelia began to believe she could actually

make a living by flying. "Someday," Amelia told herself, "I will fly the Atlantic by myself."

George Putnam became her manager and asked her to write a book about her experiences. Amelia accepted. She could use the money she made from the book to pay for more flying time. The book was called *20 Hours, 40 Minutes*, which is how long the trans-Atlantic flight lasted. George scheduled many speaking engagements for Amelia. In six months, she spoke over 100 times and gave more than 200 interviews. She also made money by letting some companies use her name to advertise their products, such as the fur-lined "Amelia Earhart flying suit." A week before her 32nd birthday, Amelia bought a used plane built for speed. She was determined to set some more records.

Races

She participated in the Women's Air Derby, the first women's cross-country race. She would fly from Santa Monica, California, to Cleveland, Ohio, over the dangerous Rocky Mountains. On August 28, 1929, approximately 20,000 people turned out to watch.

Nineteen women pilots participated in the eight or nine-day race. Some of the planes ran into trouble. Amelia's plane flipped over when she landed, but she fixed it and kept going. Some of the other planes crashed, and one of the pilots died. When the race was over, only 11 of the 19 women had completed the race. Amelia came in third, but she wasn't discouraged. As a follow-up to the race, some of the women pilots started a club. They called themselves the Ninety-Nines. By the following summer, they had close to 200 members, many of whom Amelia had recruited. Amelia was elected president of the club, and the members worked to help women pilots get jobs.

Solo Flight

On February 7, 1931, George Putnam and Amelia were married, but Amelia kept her well-known last name. One day Amelia told George she wanted to fly over the Atlantic Ocean solo. On May 20, 1932, Amelia took off for Europe — by herself. People everywhere were praying for her safety, wondering if she would make it. She ran into some difficulties. Ice

formed on the wings of the plane, causing her to have to fly at a lower altitude to allow time for the ice to melt. Then one of the gasoline tanks began to leak. Amelia flew the plane lower so she could bail out more easily if it caught on fire. She continued through the night. She had intended to fly to Paris, but decided she should land in Ireland for her safety. She brought her plane down in a cow pasture. It had taken her just 15 hours and 18 minutes to cross the Atlantic, setting a new record! A London newspaper printed, "Not America only, not women only, but the whole world is proud of her."[53]

George took a ship to Europe to meet her. They went to France, Italy, and Belgium together. They had lunch with the king and queen of Belgium who awarded Amelia with a medal. On their return to New York, they were greeted by crowds of people. President Herbert Hoover invited them to dinner at the White House. He presented Amelia with a medal from the National Geographic Society. "The nation is proud that an American woman should be the first woman in history to fly an airplane alone across the Atlantic Ocean," he stated.[54]

The Last Flight

A few years later, Amelia told George it was her dream to fly around the entire world. He

helped her to make her plans, and on May 21, 1937, Amelia left Oakland, California, with her navigator, Fred Noonan. Amelia flew over 40 hours and 4,000 miles the first week. In three weeks she had flown 20,000 miles in 135 hours. By July 1 she reached New Guinea. The plan was to go from there to Howland Island to refuel, and then on to Honolulu, Hawaii. Last stop: Oakland, California. The entire trip was 29,000 miles. All but 7,000 were done and the rest was pretty much over the Pacific Ocean. On July 2, she left New Guinea.

Howland Island was so small it was hard to locate. The U.S. Coast Guard dispatched a ship to send out signals to help them spot the island. Amelia had radio contact for the next seven hours but then went out of range. The Coast Guard crew heard short messages from her during the night but couldn't figure out her location. She couldn't hear their messages to her. At 7:42 a.m., they briefly heard her say, "We must be on you, but cannot see you and gas is running low. Been unable to reach you by radio."[55] At 8:45, they heard her say, "We are running north and south!"[56] Those were the last words the men heard from her. They knew she must be lost. They concluded that her plane

must have run out of gas and come down. More than 4,000 men on ten ships and 65 planes participated in the search. No one was ever able to find them or the downed plane.

Amelia had written a letter to George to be read if something happened to her. It said, "I want to do it, because I want to do it. Women must try to do things as men have tried. When they fail, their failure must be but a challenge to others."[57] Amelia Earhart was truly a **pioneer** of the skies who inspired many others to try hard things.

pioneer: first to do something

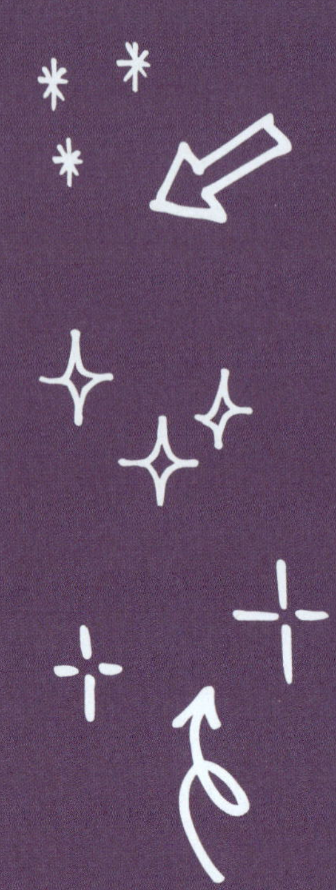

10

Helen Keller – The Overcomer

June 27, 1880– June 1, 1968	West Tuscumbia, Alabama– Westport, Connecticut

Who Was Helen Keller?

Helen Keller was born on June 27, 1880, in Tuscumbia, Alabama. Her father was a captain in the Confederate Army during the Civil War. The family had lost much of their wealth due to the war. They lived comfortably on their spacious family farm now that the war was over. In addition to running his farm, Captain Keller also edited a local newspaper, the *North Alabamian*. Helen was born a healthy child. She was the apple of her parents' eye. She learned to say words early and walked at an early age. When she was 19 months old, she became very sick with either scarlet fever or rubella. While sick, Helen had a very high fever. Not many medicines had been discovered in those days. Her parents feared she would die, but Helen recovered. However, her parents soon realized she could no longer see or hear. The fever had left Helen both deaf and blind.

The Silent Darkness

Life became very hard for little Helen. When she wanted to run, she would crash into trees, or stumble over objects and fall. She could not understand others and they could not understand her. Her frustration led her to play roughly, so other children were afraid of her. She had a bad temper and would fly into rages of kicking and screaming. Her own dog was scared of her. She once dumped her baby sister out of her cradle. She often grabbed food off others' plates. Her parents did not

know how to correct her to make her understand. Imagine what it would be like to see nothing and hear nothing! The world was a dark, lonely, frustrating place for Helen. She once locked her mother in the pantry and smiled as she felt the **vibrations** of her pounding on the door. Her mother was in the pantry for three hours. Her parents knew they had to get help.

vibrations: Feel of movement

Time to Get Help

Helen's parents took her to a famous eye doctor in Baltimore, Maryland. He said there was nothing he could do, but told them about Alexander Graham Bell, who was studying how to help the deaf. Bell was in Washington, D.C. Unfortunately, he could do nothing either, but told them about Mr. Michael Anagnos from Boston, who ran a school for the blind and deaf. It was called the Perkins Institute for the Blind.

March 3, 1887, would be the most important day in Helen's life, but neither she nor her parents knew it at the time. Mr. Anagnos sent Miss Anne Sullivan, a 20-year-old woman, to live with the Kellers and become Helen's teacher. Miss Sullivan had been blind herself as a child, but an operation had given her sight back to her. Helen could sense that something different was

going to happen that day. A spare room was opened up and aired out, and fresh sheets put on the bed. She smelled things baking. Not understanding but feeling apprehensive, Helen was not on her best behavior. Helen felt the vibrations of horses and the carriage coming. Her mother was dressed up, and she knew that meant her mother was going somewhere. She grabbed onto her mother, wanting to go too, but her father's strong hands held her back.

Helen waited quite a while on the porch for her mother to return. She had gone to the train station to pick up Anne Sullivan. When she felt the vibration of the carriage coming, she ran and stretched out her arms to embrace her mother. Instead, a stranger hugged her. Helen did not like strangers, but she was curious. She felt the stranger's face. She opened the stranger's bag, hoping for a treat. Her mother, embarrassed, took it away, and Helen started to pitch a fit. Annie took her pocket watch and held it up to Helen's face for her to feel the ticking. That quieted her down, and she followed Annie upstairs to her room.

Lessons Begin

The next morning, Helen helped Annie unpack her things. Annie had brought a beautiful doll, a gift to Helen from the children at Perkins School. Annie spelled the word doll into Helen's hand using the manual alphabet developed for the blind. Then she put the doll down and got a piece of cake. Annie spelled the word into Helen's hand while holding the cake under her nose so she could smell it. When Helen spelled C-A-K-E back in Annie's hand, Annie gave her the cake to eat. Years later, Helen said, "I did not know that I was spelling a word or even that words existed. I was simply making my fingers go in monkey-like imitation."[58] Helen wanted the doll back, but Annie wanted her to spell D-O-L-L first. Helen flew into a rage and tried to grab the doll. When she did not get the doll back, she ran downstairs, banging the door behind her. Annie thought, "We've had our first lesson, little Helen. It was only half successful. But that wasn't your fault. I was going too fast for you. But you can learn. I know you can!"[59] It would be a long, hard road for teacher and pupil.

Obedience First

Helen did not want anything to do with Annie. The next morning at breakfast, Helen began grabbing whatever food she wanted off everyone's plates. No one tried to stop her. Annie was shocked. She decided Helen would not eat from her plate! When Helen tried, Annie gently slapped her hand and pushed it away.

Helen flew into a rage, kicking and screaming. Annie picked the child up, shook her lightly, and set her sternly on a chair, holding her firmly. She put a spoon in Helen's hand, showing her how to scoop up food, and guided it to Helen's mouth. Helen threw the spoon, but Annie had her do it again. Helen was crying. Captain Keller had had enough. "I can't take any more of this," he said. Her mother followed him out of the room.

Annie decided they needed to win this battle, and it might as well be today. She locked the door. Helen began pinching Annie, and Annie would slap her gently whenever she did. Helen went to her father and mother's place, but finding them no longer there, she returned to Annie. Again, Annie placed the spoon in Helen's hand, guiding it to her mouth. This time, Helen let her do it. She finished her breakfast that morning with no more **tantrums**. Annie realized that she needed to live alone with Helen to be able to teach her effectively. Her mother and father could not bear to hear and see her cry, but it was necessary to teach her obedience. Without that, Annie could not teach Helen anything. The Kellers agreed, and Annie and Helen moved to the cottage near the big house.

tantrums: Fits

Alone with Helen

Annie drove Helen around in the carriage for a while, and moved all the furniture to different locations in the cottage so that Helen would not know how close she was to home. There, Helen and Annie fought many battles. Over the next two weeks, Helen began to change. She began to obey Annie. It was on April 5, 1887, that a breakthrough occurred. Helen was washing the dishes. Annie spelled W-A-T-E-R into her hand. Then Annie took Helen outside to the water pump, pumped water into Helen's hand, and spelled it again. An amazing look of understanding came across Helen's face. She spelled water back several times to Annie. Now, at last, Helen understood that words stood for things!

In writing her autobiography years later, Helen wrote, "Everything had a name, and each name gave birth to a new thought."[60] Then Helen pointed to the ground, and Annie spelled G-R-O-U-N-D. Helen pointed to Annie, and Annie spelled T-E-A-C-H-E-R. Helen never called Annie by any other name from that time on. Helen pointed to herself, and Annie spelled, H-E-L-E-N K-E-L-L-E-R. Helen actually smiled. She never knew she had a name before. Helen and Annie both ran to the house to find Mrs. Keller. Helen ran into her mother's arms, took her hand, and spelled M-O-T-H-E-R. Mrs. Keller's eyes filled with tears of joy. "Miss Annie, what you have done is a miracle," she cried.[61]

The rest of the day was full of exploration as Helen ran about touching things and Annie spelled the words in her hand. That evening Annie told Captain Keller, "Helen is trying to make up in one day what other children have taken six years to learn."[62] When Helen went to bed that night, she kissed Annie for the first time ever. "I thought my heart would burst with joy," Annie wrote.[63] Helen said many years later, "I was born again that day.... Now I knew my name. I was a person. I could understand people and make them understand me."[64]

A Fast Learner

Helen continued to learn quickly. Annie taught Helen to write by using a wooden writing board with **grooves** in it. She placed a piece of paper over the grooves and taught Helen to guide her pencil to form letters. She also taught her Braille, a system of reading for the blind that spelled letters with raised dots. Another world had opened up for Helen. Annie reported her progress to Mr. Anagnos, and soon Boston newspapers were writing about her, calling her the "wonder child."

grooves: Deep cuts

In 1888, Helen turned eight years old. That summer, Annie and Helen's mother took her to visit Perkins School

for the Blind. They visited Boston and the seashore at Cape Cod. Helen asked questions all the way. She was so eager to learn everything! Helen was delighted with the beach. When summer ended, Mrs. Keller returned home, but Helen and Annie stayed in Boston. Dr. Anagnos had asked Helen to be one of his pupils, with Annie still being her special teacher. She made friends quickly with other blind children and they played dolls and games together. Dr. Anagnos said, "Helen gobbles books like cookies. She cannot get enough."[65] Helen wanted to learn to speak, and Annie worked with her. At last one day, she spoke a whole sentence that Annie could understand.

More School

People were hearing about Helen's story. She met President Grover Cleveland, Oliver Wendell Holmes, a famous poet, John D. Rockefeller, and Mark Twain, who loved to make her laugh. Mark Twain raised some money to help Helen get more schooling. She and Annie went to New York to go to the Wright-Humason School. A reporter from the *New York Times* came to interview 15-year-old Helen. She was becoming famous because of the amazing **obstacles** she was overcoming. Helen even did some fun things like climbing to the top of the Statue of Liberty with her classmates. In the early 1900s, few women ever went to college, and certainly no deaf-blind women. Helen was determined to be the first one.

obstacles: Conditions that hinder progress

Helen applied for admittance to **Radcliffe** and was accepted. Few of the books were in Braille, so Annie read the books to her. Helen was learning Latin, German, and math. Helen studied day and night. In her second year, she began to write stories of her life. An editor at the *Ladies Home Journal* published them and gave Helen $3,000! That was a lot of money. Annie and Helen met an editor who helped to make Helen's stories into a book. Helen's book, *The Story of My Life*, became popular and was published in 50 languages!

Radcliffe: Women's liberal arts college in Massachusetts

In 1904, Helen graduated with honors. She wrote a second book, *The World I Live In*, describing what the life of a blind person is like. She began giving speeches to earn more money to support herself. Audiences loved her. She and Annie went on a speaking tour, traveling all over the country. In 1924, Helen started a new job that she kept for the rest of her life. The American Foundation for the Blind asked her to speak for them and raise money for the blind. She met kings, presidents, and queens, with Annie always by her side.

Annie Dies

Annie's eyesight had been failing for a few years. In 1936, she weakened and died. Helen was heartbroken. They had been together for 50 years. "A light has gone out that can never shine again for me," Helen wrote.[66] Helen knew in her heart that she must go on. Soon after, the Japanese government asked Helen to help start a school for the deaf and blind people of Japan. She gave many speeches in Japan and raised enough money for the school to open. To show their appreciation, the Japanese, having learned that Helen loved dogs, gave her a gift of an **Akita**. Helen was thrilled. She had loved dogs all her life.

Akita: Japanese mountain dog

When World War II started, many men became blinded while fighting. President Roosevelt asked Helen to visit and encourage them. She brought hope to many that they could learn to function despite their blindness. Helen continued throughout her whole life to help the **handicapped**. She met with every president, from Grover Cleveland to John F. Kennedy. In 1955, she wrote another book about her teacher, Annie Sullivan. It was made into a movie called *The Miracle Worker*, the story of Helen Keller and her beloved teacher. Helen Keller died when she was 87 years old, on June 1, 1968. She had given her life to inspire others to have the courage to overcome their handicaps and live productive lives. The night Helen died, she took out her well-used Braille Bible and ran her hands over the worn Braille dots: "The Lord is my Shepherd..." (Psalm 23).

handicapped: Physically disabled

Glossary

accommodate: Make room for.

adhere: Hold fast.

aide-de-camp: Confidential assistant.

Akita: Japanese mountain dog.

alterations: Adjustments by sewing.

altimeter: Instrument to determine altitude.

apprenticed: Taught the trade by working.

architect: Person who designs buildings.

bank: Using moveable parts of the wing to turn.

Baroness: Wife of an Austrian ruler.

bayonet: Blade attached to a rifle.

Bicentennial: 200th birthday.

buckskin: Skin of male deer.

bustling: Busy.

butler: Male servant to oversee the household.

charities: Organizations to help those in need.

coachman: Driver of a horse-drawn carriage.

collapsed: Fallen down.

Confederate: Southern.

confiscate: Take possession of.

corresponded: Wrote letters.

crew chief: Manager.

curing: Preserving by using salt.

delirious: Unaware of what was happening due to the fever.

destitute: Without money.
detected: Discovered.
devastated: Overcome with grief.
disguise: Concealing one's identity.
dismantled: Torn down.
diversion: Turning aside from an intended purpose.
drab: Dull.
epidemic: Extremely contagious sickness.
escalate: Grow.
establish: Create a government for.
feeble: Weak and sickly.
frenzied: Excited and uncontrolled.
game animals: Animals hunted in the wild, usually for meat.
gingerly: Cautiously.
grooves: Deep cuts.
handicapped: Physically disabled.
immigrated: Moved to a new country.
impart: Pass on to.
impressed: Forced to serve.
inauguration: Ceremony in which a person takes office.
inevitable: Sure to come.
inferring: Implying.
jostled: Bumped.
Kaiser: The German ruler.
lariat: Rope used as lasso.
legacy: Long-lasting impact.
loft: Space under the roof.
mangled: Wounded severely.
Mark Twain: Famous American author.

matron: Woman supervisor.

mortgage: Loan on their home.

muster: Gather.

obstacles: Conditions that hinder progress.

operas: Classical music performances.

The Order of Conductors: Organization representing train conductors in the United States.

orderly: Enlisted officer who serves an officer.

orphans: Children whose parents had died.

patrolling: Guarding.

perilous: Dangerous.

pewter: Mixture of tin and copper.

pioneer: First to do something.

plight: Dangerous situation.

politicians: People who hold elected office.

posse: Group of men whom a sheriff asks to help enforce the law.

predicted: Told her earlier.

Radcliffe: Women's liberal arts college in Massachusetts.

raiding: Surprise attack.

ratified: Approved.

recruits: New soldiers.

relief: Aid for disasters.

repel: Oppose.

scout: Person who gathers information for the army.

scouting: Exploring to gain information.

section hand: Laborer who laid and maintained railroad tracks.

sentinel: Guard.

siblings: Brothers and sisters.

silhouette: An outline against a lighter background.

skirmishes: Small battles.
solo: Alone.
stagecoach: Horse-drawn vehicle to transport passengers.
stage name: Made-up name used for performances.
stalled: Stopped running.
Stamp Act: Tax on documents.
stately: Fine.
station agent: Official and respected representative of the company.
strategic: Having a military advantage.
streetcar: Public transportation vehicle on rails.
stunt work: Difficult feats requiring great daring.
supplement: Add to.
surveying: Looking over.
tailor: One who makes clothes.
tantrums: Fits.
tavern: Restaurant and meeting place.
taxi: Move a plane on the runway.
telegraph: Machine for transmitting messages from a distance by a wire.
Tories: Those loyal to the King.
torrents: Violent rains causing flooding.
treaties: Agreements between countries.
trestles: Sloping supports used to hold up bridges.
troupe: Group of performers who travel together.
typhoid fever: Life-threatening bacterial infection.
tyranny: Oppressive control.
vibrations: Feel of movement.
Wales: Small country on the west coast of England.
yellow fever: A virus transmitted by a mosquito.

Corresponding Curriculum

The *What a Character! Series* can be used alongside other Master Books curriculum for reading practice or to dive deeper into topics that are of special interest to students.

This book in the series features animal war heroes, whose stories would incorporate well for students in grades 6–8 accompanying history, language arts, vocabulary words and definitions, as well as geography studies and cultural insights. We have provided the list below to help match this book with related Master Books curriculum.

Chapter 1: Sybil Ludington—Brave Messenger

America's Story Vol. 1

America's Struggle to Become a Nation

The Fight for Freedom

Language Lessons for a Living Education

Chapter 2: Abigail Adams—John's Dearest Friend

America's Story Vol. 1

America's Struggle to Become a Nation

The Fight for Freedom

Language Lessons for a Living Education

Chapter 3: Deborah Sampson—The Soldier with a Secret

America's Story Vol. 1

America's Struggle to Become a Nation

The Fight for Freedom

Language Lessons for a Living Education

Chapter 4: Dolley Madison—Saving George Washington

America's Story Vol. 1

America's Struggle to Become a Nation

The Fight for Freedom

Language Lessons for a Living Education

Chapter 5: Florence Nightingale—The Lady with the Lamp

Elementary World History *Language Lessons for a Living Education*

World History and Cultures

Chapter 6: Kate Shelley—The Girl Who Saved a Train

America's Story Vol. 2 *Language Lessons for a Living Education*

Chapter 7: Annie Oakley—"Little Sureshot"

America's Story Vol. 2 *Language Lessons for a Living Education*

Chapter 8: Clara Barton—The Angel of the Battlefield

America's Story Vol. 2 and Vol. 3 *Language Lessons for a Living Education*

World History and Cultures *Elementary World History*

Chapter 9: Amelia Earhart—Lady Aviator

America's Story Vol. 2 and Vol. 3 *Elementary World History*

America's Struggle to Become a Nation *Language Lessons for a Living Education*

Chapter 10: Helen Keller—The Overcomer

America's Story Vol. 3 *Language Lessons for a Living Education*

Endnotes

1. Susan Casey, *Women Heroes of the American Revolution* (Chicago, IL: Chicago Review Press, 2017) 105.
2. Ibid., 105.
3. Ibid., 109.
4. Ibid., 110.
5. True Kelley, *Who Was Abigail Adams?* (New York: Penguin Random House, 2014) 33.
6. Abigail Adams, *Letters of Mrs. Adams, the Wife of John Adams. With an Introductory Memoir by Her Grandson Charles Francis Adams* (Boston: Charles C. Little and James Brown, 1840) 40, to John Adams on June 18, 1775.
7. Kem Knapp Sawyer, Dorling Kindersley, *Abigail Adams* (New York: 2009) 41.
8. Helen Stone Peterson, *Abigail Adams* (New York: Chelsea House Publishers, 1999) 35.
9. Abigail Adams, *Letters of Mrs. Adams, the Wife of John Adams. With an Introductory Memoir by Her Grandson Charles Francis Adams* (Boston: Charles C. Little and James Brown, 1840) 122–125, to John Quincy Adams in June 1778.
10. Peterson, *Abigail Adams* 49.
11. Ibid., 54.
12. Ibid., 67.
13. Ibid., 97.
14. Edith Patterson Meyer, *Petticoat Patriots of the American Revolution* (New York: Vanguard Press, 1976) 158.
15. Ann McGovern, *The Secret Soldier: The Story of Deborah Sampson* (New York: Scholastic, 1975) 53.
16. Meyer, *Petticoat Patriots of the American Revolution,* 160.
17. Susan Casey, *Women Heroes of the American Revolution,* (Chicago, IL: Chicago Review Press, 2017) 141.
18. Jane Mayer, *Dolley Madison* (New York: Random House, 1954) 37–38.
19. Ibid., 39.
20. Mary R. Davidson, *Dolley Madison* (Champaign, IL: Garrard Publishing Company, 1966) 50.
21. Mayer, *Dolley Madison,* 113.
22. Davidson, *Dolley Madison,* 80.
23. Ibid., 80.
24. Anne Colver, *Florence Nightingale: War Nurse* (New York: Chelsea House Publishers, 1992) 21.
25. David R. Collins, *Florence Nightingale: God's Servant at the Battlefield* (Fenton, MI: Mott Media, 1985) 20.
26. Ibid., 35.
27. Ibid., 41.
28. Ibid., 42.
29. Ibid., 42.
30. Ibid., 46.
31. Ibid., 55.
32. Ibid., 56.
33. Ibid., 51.
34. Ibid., 59.
35. Ibid., 61.
36. Ibid., 67.
37. Ibid., 67.
38. Ibid., 71.
39. Ibid., 75.
40. Margaret Wetterer, *Kate Shelley and the Midnight Express* (Minneapolis, MN: Carolrhoda Books, 1990) 38.
41. Ibid., 40.
42. Charles P. Graves, *Annie Oakley: The Shooting Star* (New York: Chelsea House Publishers, 1991) 39.
43. Spinner, *Who Was Annie Oakley?* (Turtleback Books, 2002) 89.
44. Graves, *Annie Oakley: The Shooting Star,* 75.

45. Helen Dore Boylston, *Clara Barton: Founder of the American Red Cross* (New York: Random House, 1955) 37.
46. Ibid., 89.
47. Ibid., 110.
48. Stephanie Spinner, *Who Was Clara Barton?* (New York: Penguin Random House, 2014) 43.
49. Janet and Geoff Benge, *Clara Barton: Courage Under Fire* (Lynnwood, WA: Emerald Books, 2003) 189.
50. Kate Boehm Jerome, *Who Was Amelia Earhart?* (New York: Penguin Random House, 2002) 31.
51. John Parlin, *Amelia Earhart: Pioneer of the Skies* (New York: Yearling Books, 1962) 25.
52. Jerome, *Who Was Amelia Earhart?* 53.
53. Parlin, *Amelia Earhart: Pioneer of the Skies,* 52.
54. Ibid., 55.
55. Jerome, *Who Was Amelia Earhart?* 100–101.
56. Ibid., 101.
57. Parlin, *Amelia Earhart: Pioneer of the Skies,* 67.
58. Gare Thompson, *Who Was Helen Keller?* (New York: Penguin Random House, 2003) 40.
59. Lorena A. Hickok, *The Story of Helen Keller* (New York: Grosset and Dunlap, 1958) 17.
60. Thompson, *Who Was Helen Keller?* 51.
61. Margo Lundell, *A Girl Named Helen Keller* (New York: Scholastic Books, 1995) 36.
62. Stewart Graff and Polly Anne Graff, *Helen Keller: Toward the Light* (New York: Chelsea House Publishers, 1992) 30.
63. Ibid., 30.
64. Ibid., 30.
65. Ibid., 44.
66. Ibid., 68.